Make Your Own
WREATHS

Make Your Own
WREATHS
For Any Occasion in Any Season

NANCY ALEXANDER

STACKPOLE
BOOKS

Lanham Boulder New York London

Copyright © 2016 by Stackpole Books

Published by Stackpole Books
An imprint of Globe Pequot
Trade Division of The Rowman & Littlefield Publishing Group, Inc.
4501 Forbes Boulevard, Suite 200, Lanham, Maryland 20706
www.rowman.com

Distributed by National Book Network

Printed in the United States of America

First edition

Cover design by Wendy A. Reynolds
Photography by Spencer Stanton, Stanton Photography, Greenville, SC

Library of Congress Cataloging-in-Publication Data

Names: Alexander, Nancy, 1950– author.
Title: Make your own wreaths : for any occasion in any season / Nancy Alexander.
Description: First edition. | Mechanicsburg, PA : Stackpole Books, [2016]
Identifiers: LCCN 2015039132 | ISBN 9780811716192
Subjects: LCSH: Wreaths.
Classification: LCC SB449.5.W74 A44 2016 | DDC 745.92/6—dc23 LC record
    available at http://lccn.loc.gov/2015039132

Contents

Introduction

Thank you for joining me on this delightful journey into creating wreaths—from my "wild and woodsy" signature style to glamorous Christmas wreaths, and everything in between. Before we get started, I'd like to share the story of how I created my business, Ladybug Wreaths. My passion for wreaths started long before I opened my storefront and online businesses. In fact, it started when I was a young girl walking alongside my grandmother and my daddy in my hometown of Anderson, South Carolina.

As the oldest girl in a family of five, I often found myself spending several days a week at my grandmother's home. My precious grandmother radiated warmth and unconditional love as she included me in whatever creative project she undertook. She often had several projects going on at the same time.

During those weekly visits, which spanned many years, I learned how to paint furniture, sew clothing, and do counted cross-stitch. My grandmother could make beautiful works of art out of just about anything. Simple clippings from her garden turned into elegant bouquets in her strong, slender fingers.

Her hands reflected a beautiful inner strength that gave her patience to teach me to crochet scarves with tiny crochet needles. Her resilient spirit still shone in her eighties, when she realized her ceilings needed painting and didn't hesitate to climb up on her kitchen table and do it herself. I helped her dig a goldfish pond in her backyard that same year simply because she wanted to.

My daddy also nurtured my love for being outside as he found much joy working in his gardens and making our home so beautiful. If he wasn't at work in the service department of Duke Power, then you could always find him working in his yard. Our well-kept lawn was the envy of the neighborhood, and his hosta plants brought lots of attention and admiration from those who passed by.

Daddy was passionate about growing plants and taught me how to thoughtfully arrange them to create visual interest through layering the rows with plants of varying textures and colors. Of course, he didn't use those exact words as I worked beside him, but he certainly laid the foundation for how I could forever see the world in shapes and colors. He taught me how to be "wild and woodsy."

Through my time spent outside and alongside these two wonderful people, I simply fell in love with nature. I discovered that when I placed sticks together of varying lengths from different trees, I could make a creative arrangement in one of Mama's vases. So much beauty existed around me just waiting for me to notice and embrace it. My "wild and woodsy" style is a reflection of how I see the world and it speaks to my deep appreciation of the lessons I learned from these people I dearly loved.

Get Two Bonus Videos!

"How to Make a Nancy Bow"
and
"Eight Easy Steps to Designing Your Own Wreath"
To get both,
simply enter your email address:

LadybugWreaths.com/videotraining

Meet Me in Our
FREE Facebook Group!

Join me and thousands of other crafters
to share ideas and successes
every day, right here:

Facebook.com/groups/GrowWithNancy

Chapter 1
Favorite Tools, Supplies, and Materials

Tools and Supplies

One of the most important things I learned early in my career in wreath design is that the tools and supplies I use greatly affect the quality of my wreaths. It has taken years of trial and error, but now I am confident that I have found the best tools and supplies for each and every job.

Tool Basket

I'm sure every designer has her own supply basket or caddy. Mine is a basket. I function much better when my basket is organized—even down to the floral picks divided into sizes. From wire-cutters and glue guns, to pipe cleaners and wreath materials, there is a specific reason for using each particular type of material or tool in my wreaths. This information is valuable and can save you a lot of time. I have spent years doing all the research which you can benefit from, simply by reading this book.

Wire Cutters

Clauss wire cutters

Klein wire cutters

Heavy duty wire cutters

Glue Guns

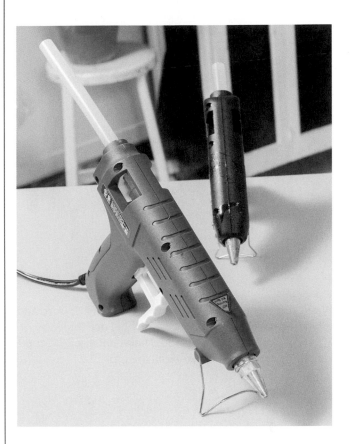

Sharp wire cutters are a necessity for any good designer if you want to take care of your arm and wrist. I use wire cutters to cut flower stems, picks, and pipe cleaners, and to trim thick branches off the backs of my wreaths, so I always have three different types on hand.

A smaller, really sharp pair from Clauss, although tiny and simplistic, allow me to almost effortlessly clip away the excess stems from the backs of my wreaths. Made of carbon steel, they are somewhat expensive, but offer a lifetime guarantee.

For those wires and stems that are too large to be trimmed with my little Clauss clippers, Klein wire cutters are an excellent alternative. Klein cutters can be purchased straight and with a slight angle, which I prefer. You can find them in the electrical section of home improvement and hardware stores or online.

When even my Klein wire cutters just aren't enough for some of my really large stems, I pull out my heavy duty wire cutters. This pair is just a little awkward, but they do the job effectively.

Just as I rely on different cutters, I also use different glue guns for different jobs.

My larger glue gun is by Surebonder. More glue flows out of the tip, making it appropriate for larger jobs or when a greater flow of glue is needed. This glue gun will drip more, and you can get burned more easily because of the quickness of the flow, but when I'm working fast—needing to get a wreath finished quickly—this is the one I prefer.

The other glue gun I use, by Darice, is small and inexpensive and can be found at any wholesale supply house. I usually purchase six to eight at a time, keeping in mind that they don't last very long. Although Darice may not have a lifetime warranty, it is by far the most cost-efficient.

This small glue gun has a fine tip and is convenient for smaller projects. I also use these for wreath-making workshops in my home studio. The flow of the glue is slower, making it less probable that a student would get burned.

I make sure to keep these two different glue guns in stock. I prefer alternating between the two sizes; using only one would make my job harder and slower. Similarly, I would be limited and inconvenienced if I were to use short glue sticks. I buy the hot-temperature long glue sticks to prevent having to reload as often.

Wired Floral Picks

Wired floral picks are necessary for affixing flowers and other decorations to wreaths. I find that I use three sizes—3", 4", and 6" (7.5, 10, and 15.25 cm)—most often, and I keep bundles of these in stock all the time.

Floral Tape

Floral tape is another necessity I keep on hand; I use it on a regular basis, in moss green, dark green, and brown. Brown comes in handy especially while working with birch. Floral tape isn't used to make my wreaths more secure. It is only used to cover picks, wire, or other work that I've done, primarily to wrap picks added to the stems of flowers and greens.

Floral tape is not sticky, but it does tend to stick to itself. Stretching it or pulling on it a bit makes it easier to wrap a stem. Make sure to always keep tension on it as you pull it around and around.

Sharp Scissors

I can't stress enough the importance of a good pair of scissors when cutting ribbon. I keep one pair of Clauss Titanium scissors and an inexpensive pair which can be replaced as often as needed. The Clauss scissors have the same lifetime guarantee as the company's wire cutters. I will warn you, however, that no matter how much you invest in them, any pair is going to dull when you are cutting wire-edged ribbons.

Pipe Cleaners or Chenille Stems

Pipe cleaners are another necessity in my studio. I use them for everything! First, a pipe cleaner is used as the hanger on the back of every wreath. Even after using glue on a stem to hold it in place, I sometimes also add a pipe cleaner to make it more secure. And larger flowers with heavy stems need to be tied in place with pipe cleaners.

My customers have told me for many years that my wreaths do not come apart . . . and they don't. Remember that a wreath hanging on a front door will often get plenty of hot sun. As the hot glue softens, materials may fall out more easily, and pipe cleaners help to hold everything in place.

Finally, all of my bows are tied with pipe cleaners instead of wire, which can be hard on your fingers.

Bostitch Stapler

The tools I've mentioned so far are those that many would expect to find in any floral designer's tool kit. One that may be surprising is a stapler. This isn't just a simple desk stapler, but a Bostitch BB plier stapler. This particular stapler is not made anymore, but there are several similar models available which will do the job. You want to find one with a long end just like mine in the above photo.

Before wired ribbon came out, tying bows was a bit more complicated. The ribbon wouldn't stand up without wire or glue, so bow loops were floppy. Reaching into a bow with the long end of my stapler, I was able to click a couple of times, inserting staples to hold loops up against each other, making them stay in place.

Today, I use it when I want to attach streamers directly into my wreaths or to attach an extra streamer or two by reaching way up inside a bow. It also comes in very handy during the Christmas season when I staple many materials to evergreen branches.

Another unique situation when a stapler saves time is when I'm creating a 2' (61 cm) table Christmas tree. It is so simple to cut a piece of ribbon 10" to 15" (25.5 to 38 cm) long, bend it in half, and staple the bent ends into a point.

I add a little glue to the stapled end and tuck it deep into the decorated table tree. It's best to leave two streamers, or tails, which flow out. Give them a little curl with your fingers and you have a nice finished look.

Wreath-Making Easel

I designed the wreath-making easel below over ten years ago. I was designing and working on wreaths that were lying flat on my work counter, which was difficult and inefficient. One day, as I worked rearranging a display in my storefront business, the back leg of an easel used for a painting fell off. It was no longer of any use to me for display, but it gave me an inspiration.

I nailed a large nail without a head into the top of the easel and propped it against my work counter. This was an awesome solution, except that it kept sliding toward me when I'd put pressure on the top of my wreath. I solved that problem and created my own custom-designed easel. A dear friend constructs these exclusively for Ladybug Wreaths. Most of my students now want their own, and they are very popular on my web site.

As you can see in the next photo, there is an adjustable hook on my easel. If I am designing a small wreath, this eliminates the need to reach up high to work on it. Instead, I remove the adjustable pin and insert it into a hole a little further down. When working on a large wreath, I move the pin up higher, so I don't have to bend down too low to work on the bottom. The slant of the easel is also adjustable, making it even easier when you're designing a larger wreath.

Door Check

I'm sure you're thinking, "What? A door check doesn't sound like a tool or a supply." Well, no, it isn't, but I consider it just as important as everything else I have mentioned.

So, exactly what is a door check? When I am designing wreaths, they hang on an easel. It makes the design process very easy, but there is always light behind my wreath. I add all the materials I think I need, and when I'm sure it is beautiful, full, and finished, the door check is next.

I hang my finished wreath on a white door in my studio. Almost immediately, any empty spot jumps right out. Against a solid white door, any imperfection stands out. I suddenly see the outside shape as it will look on a door or a wall—hanging against something solid. If the outside isn't symmetric enough or has gaping, empty spots, I have more work to do. Sometimes, I grab a few stems (usually greens) and my glue gun so I can add them as it hangs; other times, I know it has to go back to the easel for a little more intense help. This is what I have come to call a door check.

Wreath Storage

There are two other items that I find immensely helpful in my wreath making, although they are also not tools in the usual sense. When you start designing and making wreaths in your home, you may wonder where to store all of the blank wreaths you will be working on, as well as completed wreaths you are not using at the moment. That was also a problem for me when I had my storefront business.

A creative friend helped me solve that problem by installing arms made out of metal rebar or wood. They are braced in an L shape, with the short part of the L mounted against the two-by-fours in my garage. The arm sticks straight out from the wall with some support underneath, and that's where I hang all of my blank birch wreaths. A dozen wreaths or more will fit on each arm; they are out of the way, but in a convenient place for easy access and use.

When you are hanging your wreaths up high, either for storage or decoration, getting them up and down without getting a ladder out each time can be a challenge. My "wreath stick" was made thirty-plus years ago from a broomstick with a hole drilled in its end. The person who owned the shop before me had a crafty grandfather who bent a piece of really hard, stiff metal into the perfect shape for wreath hanging. A bit of hot glue keeps the wire securely in place. Sometimes the glue comes loose a bit, so I glue it back in so it'll last for another few years. If the wire was ever lost after falling out of the stick, I would be devastated! It's a keeper!

I am in the process of getting these reproduced because so many of my students want one just like mine (and in case mine ever does get lost or broken). It is perfect when

The storage arm you see in this photo doesn't have the L shape discussed (just due to a different attachment working better for this situation), but it does show you what a great storage option a hanging arm can be.

I need to reach way up on my walls to take down and hang wreaths without ever using a ladder. I don't know what I'd do without my wreath stick.

Wreath Materials

Now that you're familiar with the tools you will need to create beautiful wreaths, I'll introduce you to some of my very favorite materials for making "wild and woodsy" wreaths.

Wild Birch Wreaths

When I first started making wreaths, I used regular grapevine wreaths because that was all that was available to me at the time. I experimented with grapevine that I cut in our yard, and I learned the hard way that harvesting fresh grapevine and trying to make it into a wreath is definitely *not* easy! I even soaked that dirty vine in our bathtub hoping it would soften and bend easily. I did make a couple of wreaths for my home, but will *never* do that again.

I began purchasing grapevine wreaths, and when I finally had my own shop, it was always filled with round and oval wreaths of all sizes.

One day while working in my shop, I noticed an old, dilapidated car drive up in front. A young woman got out of the car along with three barefoot children. Before she got inside the store, I'd already met her at the door.

You see, what I spied hanging out the back of her car as she drove into the parking spot intrigued me. I was giddy with anticipation about the wild, gorgeous wreaths tied all over the car.

As we began to talk, I ooh-ed and aah-ed at what I was seeing while I was finding out about this interesting young woman. I discovered she made her wreaths from birch and beech bushes, which are plentiful in the Smoky Mountains she called her home. Her name was Ruby, and she told me she had driven nine hours with her three children and a carload of these beautiful birch and beech wreaths, looking for gift shops or florists where she could stop and try to sell her wreaths.

These wreaths, with their unique form, had sticks swooping from the top, bottom, and sides. They came in many sizes, from 10" to 24" (25.5 to 61 cm). I was impressed enough to purchase all she had that day. I was so excited about my new discovery and my new supplier, and I remember being overwhelmed by the determination that had brought her hundreds of miles away from her home so she could begin to make a living. She made something so beautiful out of nothing but natural sticks and her own two hands. The wreaths weren't tied together with wire or anything. She simply wove the vines together into a remarkable base that I had never seen before and that I couldn't wait to use.

The airy, natural, wild and woodsy look completely captured the designer within me that day. Even today, these are still the only wreaths I use, and I continue to purchase them from Ruby.

Since the birch extensions flow so far out from her wreaths, it is easy for me to follow the flow with the longer greens, flowers, and fillers that I use in my designs. A 14" (35.5 cm) wreath base can produce a much larger finished product measuring 26" to 32" (66 to 81 cm) wide. From that day on, my wreath style changed. I was addicted to wild birch wreath forms, which Ruby now creates in ovals, hearts, wall baskets, and any other shape I request.

How to Make Your Own Look-Alike Birch Wreath

Many people love the birch wreaths like mine but can't afford to purchase them. I do sell these wreaths on my web site; they are costly, but worth every penny. But did you know you can create your own copycat wreath that gives a good impersonation of a birch wreath?

It is so simple. Purchase an inexpensive grapevine wreath from a craft and hobby store or from a wholesale supplier. Break off sticks from bushes in your yard or in the woods. Add these sticks to your plain grapevine wreath, giving it a similar look to my birch wreath.

I even add extra sticks to some of my own birch wreaths when they're not quite full enough. Just run streams of hot glue down both sides of the base or stem and tuck them in around your wreath, fitting them in snugly. You'll be surprised how you can make a grapevine wreath look very similar to my birch wreath.

Honeysuckle Vine

using it to secure clay pots or other decorations, or creating bow-like loops.

As time went by, I got even more creative with these enticing vines, curling the loop way down below or up above the wreath, enlarging its size by a great deal. I just love the way honeysuckle twists around itself. It's so beautiful to me when vines grow and twist around like a braid.

Preserved Mushrooms on a Stick

I'll never forget the day Ruby walked in with something new she had harvested. It was rolled up, but thick and white, so it obviously wasn't her usual birch wreaths. She explained that while in the woods harvesting birch sticks, she spied a beautiful twisted vine of honeysuckle. Her creative side always at work, she clipped the bottom, pulling the entire vine down from the tree. Ruby thought I could do something interesting and creative with it, so she rolled the vines into tight circles and brought them to me.

Ideas filled my mind as I brainstormed what could be done with these beautiful twisted vines. As I began unrolling and pulling them apart, I examined the twisted, thicker pieces first. There were two or three vines that had curled together as they grew, making them even more beautiful and interesting. As I experimented with where I might use this honeysuckle vine in a wreath, I remember thinking how great the texture and different shades looked together! I especially loved the contrast between the lighter honeysuckle and the darker birch as I added loops and curls throughout my wreath.

That experimental wreath didn't hang on my shop wall too long. It sold immediately, when a customer realized she'd never seen anything like it before! From that day on, I have added honeysuckle in just about all of my wreaths. I've become more creative with this natural, freshly-harvested honeysuckle vine as the years have gone by. I have experimented by tying in a circle or two at the bottom,

tip I'll tell you a secret about my honeysuckle vines. I hold on to those braided sections for very special spots in my wreaths. I make sure the pieces are visible in the finished product and not tucked deep inside many greens and florals, as I want them to show their natural beauty.

Another of my favorite materials, sponge mushrooms, usually come in a pack of six and are different sizes. I prefer the large ones and wish I could purchase them in packages without the small ones, but unfortunately, I cannot. I always find uses for the smaller ones though, so they do not go to waste. The sizes you get depend on the time of year the mushrooms are harvested.

Green Sheet Moss

Mushrooms can be purchased in their natural shade, but are offered in many different dyed shades of red, brown, and green. These are real mushrooms, freshly harvested from trees and rocks, preserved, with stems inserted in their bases so that they can be added to any type of design creation. When using mushrooms, I attempt to mimic the way they grow in layers on the side of a tree.

Notice how I insert a large mushroom underneath the distressed clay pot. Mushrooms can be used as a base for clay pots as well as other objects and materials that I add to my wreath designs. The smaller ones make great shelves in areas of interest with a touch of moss and a little bird—and maybe a bird's nest. Sometimes, I use them just for contrast.

Freshly harvested green sheet moss is beautiful when used in any natural, woodsy wreath. The rich green color will last for around a year, depending on storage conditions, before it starts turning brown. Even when it turns brown, the moss is still beautiful, but I just love the bright green color of fresh moss in a newly designed wreath.

Sheet moss can be purchased from any floral supply house. It can also be purchased at craft and hobby stores, but it is not as fresh that way, and is already losing its bright green color. You should be able to find several places online that will harvest fresh sheet moss for you. It does cost a little more this way, but I believe it's worth it.

Greens and Greenery

Another thing that makes my wreaths stand out (in addition to my unique birch bases) is the large mix of greens I keep on hand and use frequently. I am never choosy about the shades of green, and I never try to match greens to each other. If you look outside, all around you in nature there are more shades of green than you can count. I strive for that same look in my unique wreaths.

I use both wired and unwired varieties in my designs, because I love the draping effect I achieve with unwired greens. In my collection are bright green stems with long branches and tiny leaf-like extensions radiating out all around, bushes that look like eucalyptus or bamboo, and grassy, curly extensions.

I constantly use taller grasses, at least 24" (61 cm) or more, in my designs. This is plastic grass, and I'm proud of it. That might seem odd, but reserve judgment until I explain about plastic greens and grasses. For years, I used thinner, synthetic grass, that would break off in my hand or give me splinters when I tried to curl it. After a wreath made with this grass had been out in damp weather hanging on a door, the grass drooped and looked terrible. Now I look for plastic grass and greens. Yes, I pay more for plastic, but I know it will last for years without fading.

A few of my favorite greens are mini ivy, English ivy, ficus leaves, ferns, and all sizes of leafy greens, as well as short-, medium-, and long-blade grasses. The different shades of green, textures, and types all contribute to an interesting, one-of-a-kind wreath design.

Succulents comprise another type of greens that are special and interesting to use. They are more expensive and can get lost in a large, full wreath very quickly, so I only add them where I'm sure they will show up well. I save these special treasures for the focal point in a wreath, using them very sparingly.

I stack my greens on a rolling cart with several shelves. I fill the shelves with supplies when I'm working on my wreaths so that I have everything at my fingertips, yet still have it out of my way when I am working at my counter.

Succulents such as these can add a special touch to your wreath. They can create a wonderful focal point.

I'm sure you'll enjoy learning how I use many of these tools on video. To see examples, watch my free video at

www.LadybugWreaths.com/videotraining

Chapter 2
Nancy's Basic Wreath

Getting Started

The first step in designing and creating a beautiful wreath is to select a blank wreath form in the size and shape you want as a base. For me, the base is always wild birch—for you, it could be grapevine. You'll find grapevine wreaths available just about anywhere you shop for floral supplies. If you have a business with a retail license, these can be purchased wholesale—sometimes for just a few dollars, depending on their size. If you cannot purchase wholesale supplies, grapevine wreaths are still plentiful and affordable at any local craft and hobby store. Don't worry too much about the way these grapevine wreaths look because you are going to be filling them with gorgeous materials.

Make a Hanger

The next step is adding a hanger to the back of the wreath. Starting with a hanger will make it easier to work on your wreath.

I always use a pipe cleaner and thread it through some of the larger stems of the wreath. When you only attach it to a smaller stem, there is a possibility it may pull out with the weight of all the objects we'll be adding.

At right: Wrapping with a pipe cleaner creates a hanger.

Add Materials to Make a Basic Wreath

Before I begin adding flowers, bows, signs, or other decorative pieces, I create what I call my "wild and woodsy" basic wreath form by wrapping honeysuckle vine and attaching greens, grasses, dried mushrooms, and a few more of my favorite materials. Here, I will show you my techniques for creating a larger basic wreath form, and then a smaller one.

Honeysuckle Vine

I'm going to start with a larger, 20" (51 cm) oval birch wreath so I can demonstrate how beautiful many loops and curls of fresh honeysuckle look. You'll enjoy learning how to work with wild honeysuckle, twisting and curling it throughout your wreath. When working with 18" to 24" (46 to 61 cm) wreaths, you'll find you can add honeysuckle in many interesting and different ways. With smaller wreaths, I use less honeysuckle, making sure I leave room for other materials such as greens and flowers.

Here is a nice, long, curly piece of honeysuckle I can't wait to put in my wreath. The end of it has a crook, meaning it will be hard to insert into the wreath form, so I begin by cutting that off into a point. With a sharp point, it is easier to insert the end into a section of your wreath.

First, insert the pointed end of the honeysuckle vine into the right side of the wreath pointing downward. Make sure to push it inside the wreath as far as possible.

Note the peculiar knot right in the twist of the honeysuckle vine. It is unique and has character, which I love. I make sure to have this knot showing right in the center of the wreath.

I'm starting with a nice long, curly piece of honeysuckle. I can't wait to add it to my wreath!

tip   When you find a knot like this in your vine, don't ever cut it out; these knots and imperfections add so much interest to the design of your wreath.

Bringing the loop up, I circle it around to the left, making sure it is not quite as high as the height of my wreath, and bring it down toward the left side. I'm not going to insert the honeysuckle into the wreath just yet, because I haven't cut it. There is not a point to insert deep into the wreath as I did on the opposite side. Leaving it all in one piece for now adds security for the loops I am about to make. There is a good spot on the left to tie or anchor it to the birch wreath. I take care of this with a green pipe cleaner. It's important to twist the pipe cleaner very tightly so that when the ends are trimmed, the vine will not pull out or come loose.

Before cutting the long piece of honeysuckle, I check to see how many more loops I can make. Visualizing a clock face, at about four o'clock, there's a perfect spot for a tight loop that could hold something.

Twisting the honeysuckle around tightly, I tie it in with a pipe cleaner and cover my work with a pinch of moss. I think a sweet bird's nest full of eggs will fit right in there.

tip As you are working, it's important to cover any pipe cleaners, wires, or picks used to secure materials into your wreath. To do that, I pinch off a tiny bit of moss and add a little glue. Then it can be tucked into the wreath covering the pipe cleaner.

Or I might shoot glue right into the wreath, tucking moss into the hot glue before it hardens. This not only covers my work, but by adding the moss and glue together, the bond is much tighter than if I were to use glue on its own.

When I tuck moss into hot glue, I never use my fingers. A long 6-inch pick works great, and saves my fingers from getting burned. With this process, I am confident that everything is there to stay.

Touches of Nature

I like to add a few "wild and woodsy" touches to my wreaths before I start adding the greens and grasses. A birdhouse or nest full of eggs, wild mushrooms, or some critters give my wreaths their fresh, natural quality.

Let's focus our attention back to the bottom center of the wreath—the focal point. I experiment a little with a birdhouse, sliding it in the bottom loop of honeysuckle and underneath the few loops that swoop down in the middle. When you want to include a darling birdhouse in a design, I advise taking the time to distress it so that it looks like you just pulled it from a tree to add it to your wreath. The birdhouse I'm using, purchased at a craft store for five or six dollars, is brand-new, light-colored wood, which is definitely not the look we want. See the sidebar on page 20 to see how to give it that worn and weathered look that fits this style of wreath.

Here are a couple of different looks you can achieve by using birdhouses and various combinations of flowers.

*H*ow to Distress a Birdhouse Using Paint, Birch, and Moss

1. I begin by mixing some grass-colored green and brown paint. The brown I usually use is burnt umber; there are many greens which look great—just don't get the duller ones. I dip a dampened sea sponge into the green and then brown paint. The I just begin dabbing on the paint without having to be really careful. This is fun, and easy!

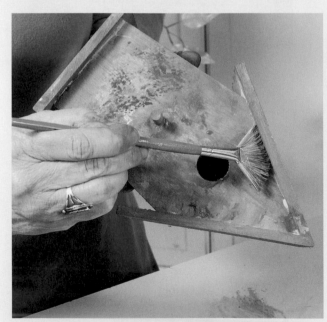

2. When the larger parts of the birdhouse are covered, I use a fan brush to reach into the tighter crooks and crevices. I don't want any of the new-looking white wood showing on this distressed house.

3. The birdhouse looks great! You can stop right here and use it as it is, or do a little more, as I'm going to do.

4. I have seen many rustic birdhouses that have different materials used for their roof, so let's try that for this one. I have some river birch trees in my backyard, and a couple of pieces of the birch bark will be just perfect to give the birdhouse the natural look I'm going for.

5. Even though the birdhouse is still wet, hot glue will still stick to it. I begin by covering the roof with hot glue, careful to not let it drip off.

My pieces of birch are rolled up—which is really great. These are going to make the cutest distressed roof ever! If you don't have river birch (as shown here), pick some pieces of bark off a pine tree. You can overlap those pieces as if you are laying a roof. That will look great, too.

6. As I lay the roof of the birdhouse with hot glue down onto a piece of river birch, it's obvious it will fit perfectly. There is just a little that I want to trim off, but not much at all.

7. Keep it laying on your counter for a few minutes making sure the glue will dry and hold before picking it up and working with the other side of the roof.

8. Well look at this! I didn't plan this, but both sides of my roof are curled back pieces of river birch. It almost looks too planned. To give it just a bit more rustic look, I add a little moss under the overhang of the roof as well as a pinch in a couple of other spots. Remember the glue is really hot, and can seep through the thin moss easily, so I still have my 6" pick handy to help tuck it in.

9. Great look, don't you think? I can't wait to add it to a wreath!

Clay Pots

Next, I audition the clay pot, and—Wow!—it looks really pretty! The clay pot is perfect, and I know that I want to add it to this wreath. As you can see, this pot does not look like "fresh" terra cotta, but instead looks like it's been out in the garden for a long time. I have used clay pots right out of my backyard—you know, the ones that look really worn, with green moss growing on the outside. The rustic appearance of these old pots is exactly what I look for. Those are the ones I like best. Realizing I couldn't always find worn and weathered pots, I decided to learn to distress them myself. I use some paint and imagination to make new pots look old. Follow along in the sidebar on page 26 for a simple process to age your new pots.

Clay pots can be narrow and tall or wide and shallow. I love using a variety of styles. When I first thought of it, I wasn't sure adding clay pots or shards would work, because they are heavy and breakable. As I started playing around with different size pots and shards, I realized I could anchor a clay pot securely into a wreath—and I *loved* that look.

I have even filled a large birch wreath with tons of honeysuckle and many pots, creating a "living wreath" to hang on an arbor in my yard. Although I didn't take the time to distress my pots for that wreath, it turned out beautifully. My flowers grew and flourished as long as I could remember to water them.

In the wreath I am demonstrating for you, the clay pot fits in the last loop of honeysuckle I wrapped at the bottom. It is secure by itself, which tells me the choice is perfect. It's important to always make sure clay pots are secure because they can be pretty heavy.

Even though it feels tightly wrapped by honeysuckle, I want to anchor my pot even more securely. The clay pot I'm using has a hole in it. If it doesn't, I get a sharp nail and a hammer and gently make a tiny hole in the bottom. (Surprisingly, you can tap a nail into a clay pot.) This hole is convenient to use to tie the pot to the wreath. With two pipe cleaners tied together, I thread them down to the bottom of the pot and pull the stems to the back of the wreath.

At this point, the pipe cleaners show in a few places, but this is of no concern because I still have plenty of moss!

As you can see, I have threaded a pipe cleaner through the hole in the bottom of the pot—I can weave both ends through the wreath, then twist them together to secure the pot.

tip For jobs when just one pipe cleaner isn't long enough, I twist a couple together. I use a very specific method to join pipe cleaners, which will not come undone no matter how hard you pull: Bend the end of one down about an inch and the other the same way. Hook these together, loop the ends around, and twist.

How to Distress Clay Pots

I use small 2 oz. (59 mL) bottles of acrylic paint purchased from my local craft store in various shades of green, and I always use burnt umber for the brown. In addition to my brushes, sea sponges are fun to use for this job; I dip them in a little water, squeeze them out, and then dip them into some paint to dab multi-colored blotches on my pots.

It is really fun dabbing the paint on clay pots because you don't really have to be careful. Anything goes! I want the pot to look rustic, so it doesn't need to be perfect.

Add more water to give the color a washed-out look; with less water, the colors are richer and darker. It's up to you to decide how you want your clay pot to look.

Another way I color my pots from time to time is with spray paint—it's fun to do and gives the pot a unique look. As always when using spray paint, it is safer to do it outside or in an area with sufficient ventilation.

Fill a plastic container with water. Spray a little of each color of the green and brown spray paints on the water— you'll find that it floats. Be sure not to spray too much, just a light film of paint is enough.

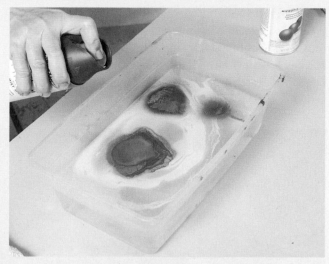

I dip pots by sort of rolling them across the top of the water in my container. The paint sticks to the pots in a variety of ways. Experiment and have a little fun with yours, just as I am with mine.

When I'm through distressing with paint and it has dried, I love going back and gluing pinches of thin green moss to my pots. I also collect other stuff in the woods such as lichen. I'm also looking for natural moss and other stuff which would grow on something you had sitting outside.

Remember . . . natural! That's what we want. Keep your eyes peeled when you're walking outside or working in your garden. You'll be surprised at what you may come across.

Weathered and distressed, these clay pots and birdhouses will be wonderful additions to a wild and woodsy wreath, especially when complemented by natural-looking floral elements.

Making Clay Pot Shards

It's just as much fun using clay pot shards as whole clay pots. (I know, that's just a fancy name for broken pieces of clay!) The ones I use didn't get broken by accident; I break them on purpose, and have become pretty good at (almost) breaking them in half.

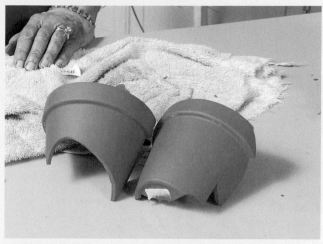

1. You will need several clay pots, an old towel, a hammer, and a large nail with a sharp point or a Phillips screwdriver with a good sharp end.

3. After I've tapped my nail into a few places, the pot breaks into pieces. The bottom is broken off in the process, but that's fine.

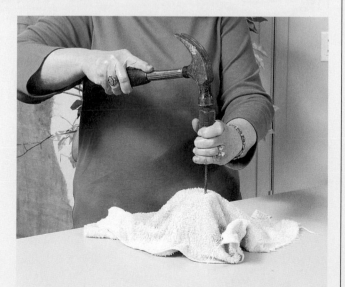

2. Make sure to cover the pot with a towel before hitting it with a hammer—sometimes it shatters and could get in your eyes. I gently hammer a nail into the pot to try to break it in half.

4. After I've broken the pot, I hold the shards up to my wreath to see how they will look. Once I add them to a wreath, I fill in with moss all around. No one will ever know that the rest of the pot is missing, but what is missing is the weight of the original pot.

Then there are times when I just hit the pot with a hammer and see what I end up with. Of course, I still wrap or cover it with a towel before I get destructive. Come to think of it, this is a great way to work out your frustrations.

I end up with some great pieces, and I usually use almost every one. I don't mind at all that people can tell they are broken. This makes it look more natural. You want your woodsy wreath to look like it's out in the garden.

A large wreath can accommodate a variety of pots and pot shards. Let your imagination be your guide!

Preserved Mushrooms

Once I have my clay pot in place, I try out one of the sponge mushrooms on a stick. I slide it underneath the clay pot, where it will act as a shelf. I attempt to mimic the way mushrooms grow in layers on the side of a tree as I tuck one tightly under the pot. It may take several attempts before finding just the right space for it to slide in securely.

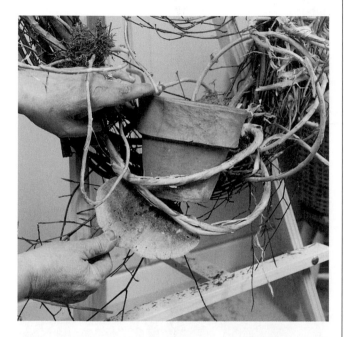

This wreath ended up with mushrooms overlapping in different directions. These are middle-sized mushrooms and they look beautiful all clustered together like this.

The fan-shaped mushroom head should rest at just the right angle to make it look as though it is growing on the wreath. To ensure the back of the wreath is attractive as well, cut the long stems of the mushrooms hanging out the back. Continue to add more mushrooms, putting them in at different angles to mimic their natural growth pattern. You'll know it's in the perfect place when it sort of wraps around in an angle like it's growing on the side of a tree.

Bird's Nest

Next, I'm going to try out the bird's nest full of eggs by inserting it into the honeysuckle loop I made on the right.

After resting the nest right on the loop, I add some hot glue and green moss to make sure it is secure. A little green sheet moss tucked underneath the nest really adds to the natural look. Remember, my goal is to make this section of our wreath look like a bird built this nest herself.

As always, hiding your work in this building process is important, so finish tucking moss in and around every spot where wire, pipe cleaners, or picks were used.

Greens

Now that we have added a few decorative touches, we are ready to start using greens. They are some of my favorite materials and help to make my wreaths stand out far above the rest. I couldn't achieve the look of a "wild and woodsy" wreath without them.

I have a large pile of greens on my work counter and more on my rolling cart. I love them all. I would like to use them all, but I need to leave room for flowers and ribbons.

A large collection of greens will inspire you to create all kinds of beautiful wreaths.

Ficus Leaves

I begin each wreath design with ficus leaves to help form the shape of my wreath.

The ficus branch is long and full, and when cut properly, it can go a long way. I usually use two ficus leaf stems in each wreath; sometimes a little more for a larger wreath.

Three major branches can be separated from one ficus leaf stem without having to add too many picks. Here, I'll probably use two stems with six sections in all. I prepare each stem by adding floral picks and tape where necessary, and begin tucking them in here and there.

Since the birch wreath extensions come out in a clockwise fashion, continue to follow the same flow with the ficus leaves, adding some toward the outside of the wreath and some coming more from the center. The longer, fuller ones are used for the top and bottom, with two on each side.

tip Gently bend each stem into a curve before adding it to the wreath. This contributes to the natural look of the wreath. Arch the branches a little, put glue on each one, and then start tucking them in.

At right is what my wreath looks like after my first layer of greenery, using ficus leaves. The darker growth down toward the bottom of each stem opens up to the new lighter growth toward the ends. The mixture of different shades between the new growth and the older growth is a beautiful contrast and really adds to the natural look we want to achieve.

You'll find after adding the first two or three stems, it may look a little unnatural. They are sticking out from the wreath more than you think they should—flowing out 8" to 12" (20 to 31 cm)—so your first instinct is to tuck them in further. Don't do it. Trust me with this one! After adding more ficus branches and other greens and flowers, you'll realize that the stem could actually have been left out even further.

How to Add Picks to Floral Stems

Floral picks are invaluable when designing wreaths and arrangements. I keep three sizes of wired picks on hand: 3", 4", and 6" (7.5, 10, and 15.25 cm). There are other sizes available, but I work very efficiently using only these sizes.

When I first began designing many years ago, I added picks to stems the best way I knew how, but they never seemed to stay as tightly as they should. I was always experimenting to find a better, more secure, way, and I finally worked out the best way to add a pick to a stem so that it will never come loose.

Lay the wired pick right beside the flower stem, overlapping a little more than an inch. (You're probably already thinking, "Well, you only have to wrap the wire around both stems, and it's done, right?" I'm afraid it just isn't that easy.) Begin twisting the wire around both stems as you twirl them around in your opposite hand. After going around both stems together only once, take the wire up above the floral pick, making a couple of turns around the flower stem only.

Begin pulling your wire back down the stem, wrapping, turning, and twirling the two stems together as you go. The key is to wrap down pretty quickly so there is enough wire left over to turn it around the pick only—this is the part below the flower stem.

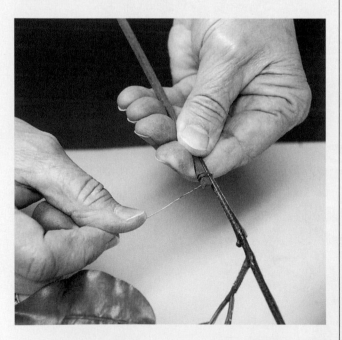

These last couple of turns around the pick finish it off in such a way that it will not come loose.

As a final touch, use floral tape to cover the wired joint.

Tall Plastic Grasses

Tall grasses are another favorite of mine. Of course, I use grasses in several different lengths in my designs, but the taller grass also helps me get the shape of my final design.

One bush of grass can be separated and spread throughout the wreath as needed. I look for wired plastic grass to use here so that I can curl it with my fingers before adding it.

When adding anything to your wreath, it's important to test to see where the stem will slide in, then pull it back out, until you're satisfied with the location. Add glue before inserting it the final time.

Grass sections are added at the top, bottom, and sides of the wreath, similar to the way I have already added ficus, with the taller pieces at the top and bottom and the shorter pieces on the sides. This gives the effect of an oval wreath, even though the base may not be oval.

Shorter Grasses

If you are following along with me, we are ready to add two more types of grasses. One has a very pretty beaded look, with tiny leaves running down each stem. The other is a lighter, lime green grass, which provides some contrast.

I insert these here and there to start filling in sections which need a little something, adding only a few stems of each so I don't fill my wreath too quickly.

We have just finished a basic wreath form. From this base wreath, you can add many different materials, as I'll be showing you in the next chapter. You'll be surprised at the different looks you can create from this basic form.

Smaller Basic Wreath

If a large wreath isn't what you need, you can create an equally beautiful wreath in a smaller size, simply by choosing a smaller blank wreath. You can still add honeysuckle in lots of different and interesting ways. As wreaths get smaller, I use less honeysuckle, making fewer loops and curls, but that doesn't mean they are any less natural or enticing.

For the smaller wreaths, I want a loop to curl up and over to the left. To make sure it shows up well, I leave a few inches between the top of the honeysuckle loop and my birch wreath. I don't want them to lie on top of each other as they would blend together too much. Once I bring it over to the left side, I tie it securely with a pipe cleaner to a branch near the bottom left side.

tip Sometimes, I don't cut the honeysuckle vine at all from beginning to end. Other times, I insert a few separate pieces and tie each end into my wreath. I love it when I find a piece that naturally curls around into a loop. I like to do something creative with these beautiful loops, like wrap them around a pot.

I attach my preserved mushrooms, as usual, but without the loops of honeysuckle I have to find a different way to attach my little bird's nest. It's fun to place the nest on top of the mushroom. The nest looks like it belongs there, and the mushroom acts as a cute little shelf.

To secure a bird's nest on top of the mushroom shelf, tie two picks together by wrapping the wires of the two separate picks around each other so they will not pull apart. That gives you a thick wire in the middle with one 6" (15.25 cm) long pick on each end. Since I don't want to insert these picks through the mushroom, I make sure they point at an angle behind the mushroom and into my wreath. Again I finish off this step with a little glue and moss. With the picks secure, I place moss on top to make sure it doesn't move.

Finally, I add my ficus leaves to finish off this smaller version of my basic wreath. I limit myself to just a few, keeping in mind that I have less space to work with and many other lovely things to add.

There is always room for a clever, personalized touch!

To learn how to create any style of wreath from
my basic wreath, watch my free video at

www.LadybugWreaths.com/videotraining

Chapter 3
Decorating the Basic Wreath

I have had such a wonderful time writing this book and having the opportunity to share my love of wreath design with you. To show you how to start with a base wreath and know you'll be able to transform it with your own unique design and decorating ideas is awesome!

You may not want to add a clay pot or a birdhouse as I did. You will be able to leave out or change any step or any element, and still end up with a beautiful wreath. Your designs will be yours, not mine.

My first goal in teaching is to show students the basic fundamentals of wreath design. I want you to know which tools and supplies you'll need and what to do with them. And I guarantee you that if you follow my instructions fully, your beautiful creations will still be around—still strikingly unique and gorgeous—long after other wreaths are worn and falling apart. I show you exactly how I design and construct a wreath, and you are welcome to follow these instructions as long as you like.

But, often, something magical happens along the way. One day, as you are following my step-by-step instructions, you'll begin to wonder how it would look if . . . .

If you added a different type of greenery would you still end up with a beautiful wreath?

If you cluster your blossoms together in a different section on the other side of your wreath, will it be pretty?

If you add honeysuckle in a different way could it support that sweet bunny you purchased a while back to add to a wreath one day?

When these "ifs" start running through your mind, that's when I know I have done my job; I have taught you enough wreath design basics that you have begun to find something within yourself you never knew was there.

It's your God-given gift: it's your style.

That's my goal as I begin teaching you design through this "how to" instructional book. I am just as excited as you, knowing that you'll find and develop your gift lying deep within. You are watering and nurturing your gift as you read through my book, just as you do beautiful flowers in a garden which are about to burst into full bloom.

I get so much pleasure watching my students blossom and succeed as they reach for the stars. Their thank you notes, testimonials, and praise fill my heart.

Congratulations. You are well on your way to becoming an artisan and a designer. You've taken a new path, a new course—one that will see you creating gorgeous designs with your own two hands.

Morning Glory Wreath

My wreath base is ready. It is filled with grasses, honeysuckle vine, and fresh green moss. This next part is fun!

I'll start with a large wreath base, leaving a lot of room for creativity. Sometimes being creative is a much simpler process than you might think. Spreading one large bush of morning glories throughout this wreath is a quick and easy process that allows beginners, as well as experts, to create a colorful wreath quickly without spending a lot of time, effort, and money. This is also a great wreath-making method if you don't want to use a bow.

We all hate to spend too much on our wreath-making supplies, but there are times when a large, expensive bush can end up costing less than several inexpensive greens and flowers. I am very careful when purchasing expensive flowers, especially bushes. I normally only purchase a very costly bush if it will be enough to spread

Completed Simple Morning Glory Wreath

throughout my wreath, giving it a full, lush look. That way, I don't have to spend money on a lot of other accent flowers and additional greens.

Make sure the bush you select has some trailing stems in various lengths—short, medium, and long. A nice bush such as the one I'm using in these photos practically fills up this wreath.

Predicting how anything will look when getting started, even for a seasoned veteran, is nearly impossible. The finished wreath is often a surprise, even to its maker! Keeping that in mind, the first thing I always do is hold a bush or stems of flowers up against the center of my wreath to get a view beforehand. Experiment a little to ensure you'll be happy with the finished product.

This particular bush of flowers has long flowing stems with sweet blossoms and leaves spread along each stem, resembling vines. When holding the bush against my wreath, I notice one stem curling over to the left, up and around the top. There is another long, double stem hanging down elegantly, curling out the bottom. That's exactly the way I want this bush to look when I add it to my wreath design.

Cut the branches off and spread them around in your base wreath just as I am doing. You could use this bush all by itself, keeping it simple and beautiful, or add a few smaller, focal or filler, flowers. The choice is up to you.

This isn't a quick process. Even though I am an experienced designer, I sometimes spend quite some time choosing the right flowers. I don't stop until I'm sure the flower combination is perfect and my colors pop. Then I can begin to place the flowers in among the morning glories to create a full, gorgeous wreath.

tip It is important to position flowers so they look most natural, as if they are emerging from one center point, similar to a bush. Arrange them so they seem to be live flowers growing from one plant. Your design will look much more natural and appealing as you spread the stems throughout your wreath in this way.

Hydrangea Wreath with Natural Burlap Bow

This natural, woodsy wreath is filled with spiky, pink delphiniums accenting the pink/green hydrangeas. Blue hydrangeas add additional contrast, making the softer colors pop. The addition of hops, with its classy, flowing pods, gives this beautiful design a soft look. A double ribbon bow of natural burlap is a perfect, low-key finishing

*Completed
Hydrangea Wreath*

touch for this colorful wreath. This stunning wreath would look beautiful with any decorating style. A wide selection of greens makes this one look full and scrumptious.

We begin again with the large wreath base with honeysuckle and a clay pot that we used for the Morning Glory Wreath. There are so many different looks that can be achieved from this same 20" (51 cm) oval wreath!

First, we add a beautiful full, single ribbon bow of burlap and attach it to the wreath. Next, two smaller wired green mesh ribbon bows are tied and inserted into each side of the burlap bow. This gives the impression of a double ribbon bow without having to hold both ribbons in your hands at the same time. In other words, this is a secret way to make others think you have tied a double ribbon bow. We'll keep it just between us that it is really three bows. Refer to Chapter 4 for step-by-step instructions on tying and attaching a variety of bows and streamers.

Next we will choose the flowers from the colorful stock in my workshop. My work counter is covered with many beautiful flowers in some of my favorite colors. I really love this part of floral design!

I chose this bush of hot pink and soft pink flowers, but am only interested in using the hot pink for this wreath. I often choose to use one or two particular blossoms out of a full bush of flowers, so please don't think you must use all the flowers from a mixed bush at one time. All I need to do is clip off the pieces I want to use and save the remaining pieces for another wreath.

This beautiful bouquet includes pink and orange. I don't know if I'll be using the orange, but I do love the way the colors play against each other. I often see people hesitate to use pink and orange together. In my opinion, as long as you use the right shades, the colors look beautiful. For example, I avoid using burnt orange, or a rusty orange with more brown or red in it, when I am going to be combining it with pink. (By the way, have you noticed how striking my orange top is beside this bouquet of blossoms? I chose this on purpose—not because I love the top so much, but because I love the striking contrast!)

I'm calling this a hot pink, but if you'll notice closely, the shade has a little salmon touch to it. When looking at the pink/green hydrangea lying right beside it on my counter, pay special attention to the way that shade of salmon is picked up in both.

In all my designs I like to have some spiky flowers along with the larger and fuller blooms. The spiky flowers, the salmon pink ones in the previous photo, help me pull more color to the outside of the wreath. This keeps me from loading up the center of my wreath with color and helps the wreath stay balanced. I know you've seen wreaths like that before. They are large, but don't quite look as large as they could, because all the color is concentrated in the center.

Another thing I want you to be aware of—you often hear designers say they use odd numbers of flowers such as three or five, but I don't pay any attention to that. I add flowers to my wreath in such a way that the colors flow throughout, giving the design a cohesive look. I always start with larger flowers. They will take up the most space in my wreath. So, the first blossoms I choose in this particular wreath are hydrangeas. Using these gives me a chance to spread my large blossoms around so they look best in my wreath design. I'm sure you can tell when looking at my wreath designs that hydrangeas are probably my favorite flower.

They can be purchased in all shapes, sizes and colors. The hydrangea bushes I normally keep on hand come in several colors: blue, lime green, hot pink, soft pink, and red. The size of the flower heads varies according to the price and quality of each bush. I encourage you not to walk away from a beautiful bush of hydrangeas just because the head of the flower looks small. You are probably saving money and there are surely places where they can enhance your wreath.

Likewise, don't walk away from a hydrangea bush with heads that are too large. If the colors are pretty, I often cut the flower head into two or three sections and attach picks to them. Cutting the heads makes it necessary to use them just a little closer to your wreath. You can always bring other flowers away from your design to give it a full look.

Adding large hydrangeas to a wreath can be very charming, but close attention should be paid to how they are arranged. Normally, I don't go all the way around my wreath with a larger flower, but there are always exceptions. You might find yourself working on a really large wreath that needs many large flowers to make it look full enough.

When using large flowers like hydrangeas, I often cluster them together at the bottom. It's very attractive to group them together as a focal point.

In the following photos you'll see that I begin experimenting a little with the hydrangeas I'm going to use. I have three pink/green and two blue hydrangeas. I'll cut the long stems off a little, then bend them into a curve before putting them in the wreath. This gives them a more natural look. I am inserting these stems in different spots to decide where they will look the best. I suggest you try it this way also, at least until you become more experienced; even when you develop your own style, and you will, you'll still find yourself changing your mind at times. Feel free to experiment and have some fun, and then step back and look at your design.

So, in this instance, I decide that I want one bloom to be pointing up and one to be curled down and around. I step back to get a better view of the wreath and realize I'd like to rearrange things. I think the arrangement of the pinks at the bottom and blues at the top can be adjusted to look more attractive, so I simply reposition them a bit, moving the blue hydrangeas side by side at the bottom.

I hold up several hydrangea stems to see where I might like them to go. I know, you probably want me to tell you exactly where they should go and then describe why I made that choice. Unfortunately, this is something no designer can give you hard and fast rules for. You need to learn to develop your eye of design by trying each stem in different spots. When you do come up with the right spot for each stem, you'll know immediately. This is something that comes with experience. And, in case you're wondering, I still experiment and move them around myself (after all my years of experience), until I am pleased with their placement.

I wish I could give you an exact, technical reason why I changed the flowers and colors around, but I can't. Through practice, you will develop an eye for this yourself. It will come with time, as you begin to see your own style emerge.

I am going to experiment with a green hops spray next. I actually love this spray just as it is, all together in one large stem. One thing that always draws my attention to a stem like this is the way the flowers drape. Don't get me wrong, I often use wired stems and purchase very few without wire, but this is one of those exceptions. This airy, wispy look can add so much to any natural, wild and woodsy design.

Hops flower pods have a beautiful shape as they flow loosely from the front of the wreath. Make sure to arrange them so that they can dangle loosely out of your wreath.

I don't want to cut this stem, but it is necessary. I am careful not to lose the flowing look as the stems are added.

The branch I'm adding in the center just does not want to stay in place. It's very easy to grab a small piece of wire or a pipe cleaner to tie it onto the honeysuckle loop. Remember, always cover these areas by gluing on a tiny pinch of green sheet moss.

tip A word of caution when using hops, or any other larger and more expensive stems: In the past, I have cut up a stem like this so much that it loses its airy, flowing look. It's important to keep this look in your design and not make this same mistake. You may have to cut a large stem some, but be careful not to lose its drapey effect.

I cut a few more stems from the hops spray and find a couple of perfect spots for them. I then add a long stem so that it is hanging out of my bow on the left side and decide one would look beautiful at the bottom of the wreath, threaded in between the blue hydrangeas. I really like the flower head hanging out the bottom.

When a wreath looks just a little dark, as mine does now, I am inspired to add some lighter shades of green. I am always on the lookout for lime greens and yellow greens to use as brighteners.

These can be added to your wreath design very quickly. If the stems are short, you may need to add picks to them.

tip Before trying to reach into a bush with your wire cutters, simply bend each one out and away from the base. It's quick and simple and it allows me to cut up a bush very quickly.

Starting on the left side, I tuck the greens in here and there. A piece coming out from underneath the bird's nest would look great. I also want one coming out of the bottom of the wreath, a perfect place for a loose stem of this green leafy filler. I tuck some more pieces of light green in at the top and a few other places throughout my wreath.

After finishing up with the leafy green bush, I experiment by holding up different flowers, fillers, and colors to see what I should add next. I start by adding an orange filler flower, as well as yellow and white ones. Just by holding them up, I could see that the white flower would give my design more color contrast, which is exactly what it needed.

It's time to add some color that will flow out from the main circle of the wreath. This two-tone pink bush is just perfect, but I'm only going to use the deeper shade, since it looks great with my hydrangeas. I'll clip off the stems I want to use and save the remaining flowers for another wreath.

It doesn't matter how long you've been making wreaths. You will always benefit from experimenting. Even I have to try out different materials before I can tell for sure if I like it or not. Sometimes, you need a brighter color, like the hot pink, to make it pop. When bringing in a bolder color, make sure to spread it somewhat consistently throughout your wreath. As I step back to get a good view, I realize that the pink was definitely what was needed to brighten things up.

Don't forget to step back and look at the whole wreath as you work. Doing so will help you see that all the elements are in balance.

I am ready to add those delicate, tiny white flowers I was checking out earlier. They are perfect! They flow out of the wreath pretty far, so I want to put some with shorter stems right in the middle also. It looks really sweet to add one right next to the bird's nest. Another piece looks great wrapped around the clay pot. Notice how I'm spacing them. You want them to flow out of your wreath rather than be tucked tightly inside. The whites should be used as we used the pinks, making sure not to clump them together in one spot.

tip It's important to add pieces of the materials used in your design right into the center of the bow. This helps your bow blend in with the entire design rather than looking like an afterthought. These bows look like they don't quite fit in, and you don't want that.

A big part of my natural, wild and woodsy style is the way I use critters! I am a firm believer in adding critters—birds, hummingbirds, frogs, ladybugs, grasshoppers, nests with eggs, and so forth—to any wreath design. I plan to add three different birds to this wreath. Let me show you how it is done.

The hummingbird is the simplest of all. It is on a long wire, which I tuck into the side of my wreath. After all, it looks more real if this hummer is buzzing above the bird's nest, don't you think?

The next bird is going to be fun and easy. There is such a simple way to tie it onto the thick loop of honeysuckle draping across the front of my wreath. There are no wires to tie on this sweet bird, but that's okay, I'll fashion my own.

First, make a hole in the bottom of the bird with the pointed end of a floral pick—the bird is made of Styrofoam, so it will slide right in.

Shoot a little glue into the hole, bend a pipe cleaner in half, and insert the folded end into the hole. Let it dry for a minute or two, and it's there to stay.

Tie the bird on with the pipe cleaner, add a little more glue and a touch of moss, and she is secured forever!

When adding a bird to a branch, I always add a touch of moss. This does double duty, hiding our pipe cleaner and making it all look more natural, too.

Notice how I draped and glued another piece of moss over the rim of the pot. Cute, huh?

We already have two birds, but I think I'll add a third to the edge of the clay pot. I just fold up a thick piece of moss, and glue and tuck it over the opening. For this bird, just add lots of glue and hold it in place. It will sit on the clay pot and the moss and, when dry, it will be securely attached.

This wreath turned out to be such a beauty! And I guarantee, if you follow these simple steps, you can do this, too!

tip There are many who hang their wreaths on glass doors. To make sure those doors don't get scratched, always cut picks and stems very close to the back of the wreath, and then cover all the rough areas of your work with pieces of green sheet moss.

Geranium Wreath

Geraniums are beautiful flowers and are great to use in the spring and summer. I already know I want to use geraniums in this wreath because they would look beautiful as the focal point, coming right out of the clay pot.

I like being able to add a whole bush of flowers still attached to their original stem. The most attractive place for a nicer, more expensive bush like this is inside the clay pot, flowing out and bringing life to the center of my design. These are larger flowers—although not as large as hydrangeas—and you will only need some accent flowers to complete your design.

*Completed
Geranium Wreath*

I have already picked some of my favorite flowers to accent this geranium wreath. These flowers are pink or rose-colored geraniums, grape hyacinths, and a green/pink hydrangea.

I begin with the same large basic wreath we started with. I've removed everything from the first wreath except the basics I began with: honeysuckle, greens, and some accessories like the birds, bird's nest, and clay pot.

A double ribbon bow with streamers is the first thing I want to add. The streamers will be woven throughout the bush, making it nearly impossible to see that the pink geranium heads are still connected to their base stem.

I always keep desert foam bricks in my shop. They are perfect to use when anchoring flowers to any type of pot. I don't use them often because I am not designing many arrangements anymore. But, when I need them, nothing else will do. You can find this material at floral supply houses and craft and hobby stores.

Cutting Floral Foam Bricks

I'll tell you a little secret here. Many people use serrated knives to cut desert foam and Styrofoam, but this can make quite a mess of crumbs.

I have found the perfect solution—a hacksaw blade. (You can buy your own or "borrow" your husband's.) It cuts through so easily and doesn't leave the mess of crumbs that a serrated knife produces. You still get a few gritty crumbs, but not nearly as many as you would when using a blade with larger teeth.

Even though you'll end up with that fine grit between your fingers and all over the counter, using foam bricks makes floral design so much easier and is definitely worth the hassle.

Start by trimming the foam corners so you can push it tightly into the round clay pot. I use a screwdriver to make a hole in the center for the flowers, and then add glue around the edges of the foam so it stays securely in the pot.

Cut off the excess flower bush stem and try it out in the pot. If you like the way it looks, take it back out, generously add hot glue directly into the hole, and push the flower bush stem in.

I start experimenting with different flowers to see which ones to I want to use next. Because the geranium bush has quite a few blossoms, I don't need to use as many additional flowers, so I decide on one or two hydrangeas and a few smaller flowers.

I have a gorgeous deep purple grape hyacinth bush I think would look great. It will really bring this design to life with an additional pop of color. It is perfect—not too large, but very rich looking. I pull its branches apart so that it's easy to go in a circle and clip its stems off one by one. I put one stem above the bird's nest (after attaching a pick so that it sticks out a bit further than the nest) and another right beside the bow.

It takes a bit of fiddling to get everything the way I want it.

I have one more stem of the hops that I used in our first wreath. I love it so much I think I'll add it to this wreath, also.

The next filler I want to use is some yellow Queen Anne's lace. These flat, delicate flowers are a perfect addition to spots that seem a bit empty. They will look especially attractive and help to fill in the holes because of the extra grasses attached to them. I first add a stem to the very top of my wreath. When I add fillers to the top, I insert them in closer to the back of the wreath than the front.

tip Adding filler flowers is one of the more time-consuming parts of designing a wreath. Completing your creation with a variety of small fillers may not seem to be worth the time, but I believe it pays off in a richer, fuller, and more luxurious wreath. It may be difficult to find empty holes, but if you look around enough you can always make these fillers work.

After I've added all the Queen Anne's lace, I go through the wreath adding hot pink filler. It seems to brighten up the whole design. I think a short stem of this pink filler would look great sticking out of the bow, along with a little bit of light green grass.

I think that the wreath needs some more green, so light green filler grass added here and there throughout my wreath is perfect. Working my way around, I keep looking for empty spots to fill with this pretty lime green grass.

When my wreath design seems to be complete, I take the time to closely examine each area to make sure there are no gaps and no areas with too much or not enough color. Remember my door check?

As a finishing touch I have to add my signature ladybug. Can you find her?

A Few More Designs

It is amazing that a simple change of flowers can give the basic wreath so many different looks. I have shown you three wreath styles in detail, but I also want to show you a few more of the many ways you can use the same base to create different designs to adorn your home or give as gifts.

A colorful wreath like this one is a great way to welcome the spring and summer seasons. This beauty started as most Ladybug wreaths do. The base is a 16" (40 cm) wild birch wreath. Without the many loops and curls of thinner, freshly harvested honeysuckle vine, this wreath would seem a little stiff. In my wreath designs, you can normally find larger flowers, medium flowers, and smaller, airy blossoms that bring color out from each wreath design.

This one has a bird's nest filled with eggs resting on a sponge mushroom. A pretty bird is perched on the side, seemingly guarding her nest. A full bow made of #40 burlap and green striped ribbon has flowers and greens tucked in and around so that it doesn't stand out too much—and I always *love* long ribbon streamers. You'll find yellow Queen Anne's lace and pink carnations tastefully placed throughout. Yellow and green cherry blossoms have long stems of tiny blooms that bring color out away from the wreath, as do the small pink and white morning glories. It's never a good idea to have all the color right in the center circle of a wreath. I love the airy tendrils of color that flow in all directions. And, of course, you will find several types of grass, mini-leaf variegated ivy, and ficus leaves.

This beautiful oval wreath has a different look than most. This is achieved with greens which seem to hang down away from the wreath. You'll find my staple greenery, ficus leaves, but in addition there is a drapey stem of leafy greens which seem to curl and flow downward. Four pink and light pink hydrangeas are spaced at the top and bottom, adding to the oval look. For the medium flowers, I used a white carnation. And, of course, there must be a smaller stem of blossoms that flow out and away from this beauty. This one is made of two shades of morning glory stems.

Notice this wreath was designed with a cluster of flowers and greens at the top and then a cluster of flowers, greens, and the bow at the bottom. Don't ever be afraid to leave part of the woody section of your wreath base showing. You don't have to cover every single section of the wreath. I actually like it better when it is not quite as full.

Fresh honeysuckle vine has many loops twisted together, adding to the airy look that I love so much. A beautiful double ribbon bow with long, curling streamers brightens a wreath which could be a little dark. Both #9 wired ribbons are stiff and make beautiful loops. The green burlap and gingham checked cotton look beautiful together.

Blues and yellows are often used together in floral design. There are many similar flowers found in this wreath, as in many other wreaths, but yet it looks completely different. The way the flowers are placed and the colors used make such a difference in the finished look. Blue hydrangeas, yellow cherry blossoms, and pink and white morning glories enhance the spring and summer colors found in this one. Oh, and I definitely cannot leave out the tiny pale yellow filler spread throughout. This is another filler that adds to a loose, airy look rather than a stiff, tight look.

I believe what I like the most in this beauty is the double ribbon bow with very long, curling streamers hanging way below the wreath. Those streamers—along with the greens and filler flowers coming out the top—give this wreath an oval look, although it is not on an oval base. Starting with a round base, it is possible to achieve any type of shape in your design just by the way your flowers, ribbons, and greens are placed.

I love this wreath! It is very large but will still fit on a normal 36" (91 cm) front door. This one began on a 20" (51 cm) oval birch base.

I want you to pay special attention to something about this one. There aren't any really large or expensive flowers. Do you see any? Actually, most of the blossoms and blooms in this exceptional wreath came from floral bushes. When you purchase bushes of flowers instead of more expensive hand-wrapped single stems, check to make sure the quality of all flowers and greens are good. If so, then you'll save a lot of money on your supplies!

There are pink hydrangeas, but the heads have been cut in half, purposely making them much smaller. There are hot pink Gerbera daisies, airy pink filler flowers, and a medium pink blossom. Notice some of these medium to smaller size flowers do not even have a specific name. I call them blossoms and blooms when writing a description of them. You'll also find yellow Queen Anne's lace with lots of grasses attached to each bloom and plenty of tiny star filler flowers.

Of course, there is a mix of greens as in all my special wreaths. Don't be afraid to add a mixture—that is just one of the special details that makes my wreaths stand out far above the rest.

Now, I just cannot leave out this beautiful bow! This is tied as a double ribbon bow. Plaid wired pink and green burlap and green and pink quatrefoil wired ribbon make a scrumptious bow! Yes, I know it is strange to say a bow and its ribbons are scrumptious, but to me they really are! And the four very long, slightly curled streamers just add more length and style to this very special door wreath.

Several years ago, I custom-made this wreath as a special order. My customer wasn't sure at first what she wanted, but she had a fairly large collection of blue and white china displayed in her den, where she wanted to hang the wreath. I asked her if she had an extra cup and saucer that she wouldn't mind if I attached to her wreath however possible. I had come up with an exciting idea, but didn't tell her ahead of time. When I sent her photos of the finished wreath, she was ecstatic.

As you can see, I took advantage of the tendrils from one of my stems—the one attached to the blue berries. First, I glued the cup to the saucer. Then, I added a large sponge mushroom to form a sort of shelf and glued the saucer to the mushroom. Knowing the cup and saucer would not stay attached by glue only, I used some of the wired, curly stems to secure it. One is wrapped around the saucer, one around the base of the cup, and another around the cup handle. An antique spoon I picked up at a yard sale was glued to the inside of the teacup with a pinch of moss for security. Two Celestial Seasonings teabags were tucked in behind a beautiful white magnolia. Later (not in the photo), I opened a teabag and glued it to the side of the saucer with the string hanging down.

I could not have made this lady any happier! When you have a wreath idea that excites you but you are not sure how to make it work, just give it a go. There is almost always a way to add items to any type of character wreath.

Adding Accents

Once you have mastered the basic wreath form and learned how to decorate it using flowers, bows, critters, and so forth, you can change its style very easily simply by adding a variety of accessories found in any craft store. I picked out several to show you how I add objects to my wreaths. These are demonstrated on a small basic wreath form, but you can use these techniques on any size wreath.

Welcome Wreath

A large and colorful welcome sign will let your guests know you're happy to see them. This large sign will cover the center of my wreath. It may seem too large, but it creates a great focal point, so don't shy away from this size. When using an accessory this large, though, I make sure to add it first. Then I can position flowers and ribbon around it so as to not hide the words.

This one is simple because I can thread a pipe cleaner through one of the loops in the chain. I purposely choose to hang it so that it will be a little off center and crooked.

When it comes to attaching a large or bulky object to your wreath, it is best to affix it securely on at least one side, as well as the top, to make sure it is anchored properly. In addition to securing the chain to the top of my wreath, I also look for a tiny hole or loop where the chain is attached to the sign and use that to insert a wire or pipe cleaner. On this wreath, there is a large loop of honeysuckle vine; it is sturdy and the perfect place to attach the sign's chain.

I have never found a single object that I couldn't securely affix to my wreath design. There have been times, however, when I was sure I wouldn't be able to figure out a solution. If I had listened to my instincts, I probably wouldn't have even tried. Once you get started, there is always a way! Just remember that and don't give up before giving it a try.

A warm and welcoming wreath—perfect for spring!

Angel Wreath

I found a sweet wooden angel, so I remove the welcome sign to try her out. Just this slight change gives the base wreath a completely different look.

Keep your eye out for any elements that can become a focal point. You never know what you might find!

The angel is simple to attach. She is also on a chain and has several little wire adornments. I can use any of these wired areas to help me anchor her in different spots.

Fisherman's Wreath

Now, for an even more dramatic transformation—a fishing wreath that is perfect for a lake house or a cabin in the woods or mountains.

Some signs, like this one, are on wooden stakes. On occasion, I cut them off (I have my own cordless, battery-powered mini-blade saw for this purpose), but here I'm going to leave the point hanging out from the bottom of my wreath because I like the way it looks.

To attach this sign to the wreath, simply find an open spot and slide the stake down into the wreath as far as desired. It is secured tightly and will probably never move, but I never take a chance, so I'll also glue it and tie it in wherever I can.

To continue the fishing theme of this wreath, I find a couple of large Styrofoam fish to add. I insert each fish at a different angle on the left side so they look almost like they're swimming through the water.

The fish don't have chains or wires, so to secure the fish to the wreath, you'll have to use your imagination and be creative with the tools and materials available to you. Because of the angle, I insert my larger fish first; it's easy to tie a pipe cleaner around the tail of the fish and secure it to a stem in the birch wreath.

The same can be done for the smaller fish. Since these fish are Styrofoam, you can even poke a hole through their tails to stick a pipe cleaner or a pick as we did for the little bird we added to an earlier design. This guarantees those fish aren't going anywhere.

What fisherman wouldn't want this unique creation on their front door?

Monograms are becoming more and more popular. Adding a monogram to a wreath is simpler than you might imagine. I paid someone in my hometown to cut out and paint my letters for me. You should be able to find them in most craft and hobby stores. They are also available at many wholesale floral supply companies.

Looking closely at this wreath, you can see how simple it really is. I have used about seven different types of greens, a mushroom, nest and bird. The bow is spread open pretty wide at the top—making sure that it doesn't cover my monogram. To attach the monogram I used two small, closed eye hooks, twisting them into the wreath. It will never come loose, because it is so securely fastened. And, of course, many loops of fresh honeysuckle vine are used as accents. I only used thinner ones so as not to take away from my wreath.

I love designing "Welcome Home, Baby" wreaths! They are basically made on my same birch base with a mix of greens. I do not, however, add honeysuckle vine to these. The letters are found in big box stores like Walmart and are made for toddlers to play with in the bathtub. They are soft, so it's easy to slide a pick inside with some glue. I have used rattles and pacifiers, and I love rubber duckies in different colors. Even bow clips for baby's hair look really cute. Just go shopping in the baby section and use your imagination.

There is one thing that makes this wreath unique and special: a monogram. I purchased some oilcloth in different colors and patterns and cut it into strips. My friend monograms them for me. It isn't even a part of the bow. This can also be done on regular ribbon; it doesn't have to be oilcloth. One end is tied onto a floral pick and taped, and then inserted underneath the bow with glue. This one says "It's a Boy." I have made others with "Welcome Home, Baby" or the baby's name and even birthdate. New moms love these for baby's nursery!

Fruits and Vegetables for all Seasons

Fruits and vegetables of all kinds can make a beautiful and welcoming wreath for a front door or a kitchen or dining area—and it's so easy to change with the seasons for a completely different look.

Adding any type of artificial fruit, pumpkins, or gourds to a wreath is easy. Simply make a hole in each piece with the sharp end of a pick or a screwdriver. Add hot glue to the hole and insert a 6" pick. Now, you have fruit on a pick! Cut the wired end at an angle, add glue down both sides of the pick and a little on the end of the fruit, and insert it into the wreath. This process assures it will be secure.

You may need more than one pick for larger fruits such as a pineapple. In most cases, because the pineapple is so tall and a little heavier, it should be anchored at the top also. It's easy to tie a pipe cleaner or wrapped wire around one of the pineapple leaves, secure it to a section of the wreath or a honeysuckle loop, and cover that with a pinch of moss. To secure it even more, you can find a few spots to shoot some hot glue, and even tightly tuck in a mushroom underneath the piece.

For longer pieces of fruit, such as bananas or cucumbers, stick a pick right into the end, and you can insert it into your wreath like it's hanging down from the fruit cluster.

For grapes, tie the wire of a pick around the leaves on its stem and add some floral tape, then insert the pick and let the grapes dangle a bit. I like the way the purple bunch looks below the mushroom, and the green cluster right above it!

tip Adding fruit to a wreath can sometimes be tricky, because they add so much weight. A pineapple is usually one of the heaviest pieces. If yours is really heavy, get a Phillips screwdriver and hammer it into the bottom in a few spots. If there is sand inside, you can simply pour it out. If rocks have been used to weight it, however, there is nothing you can do to lighten it short of major surgery.

There isn't much room left for pieces of larger fruit. There is one little gap in between the carrots and the banana. The wide end of this purple eggplant wouldn't fit, but if I turn it around and add a pick to the stem portion, it slides right in and fits perfectly. Tuck a few petite pears into some empty spots, and this lovely fruit and veggie wreath is complete.

During the fall, the large pineapple we used can be replaced with a pumpkin. The pumpkin is added in the same way as the other fruit, with a 6" pick and some hot glue. Pumpkins show up well with gourds and even other fruit surrounding them. Different shapes, sizes, and colors look bountiful during the fall season.

Cornucopia

Another fall favorite is a cornucopia filled with a pumpkin, fruits, and vegetables.

Attaching a cornucopia to the curved inner section of a wreath is easy. Make sure to have it curling around the curve of the wreath, with the smaller tip pointing up and the open end of the woven cornucopia in the bottom center of the wreath. Thread pipe cleaners through the woven material in at least two sections so you can tie it to your base wreath. This assures it is there to stay.

The cornucopia adds so much brown to the wreath that I add more ficus leaves around it to give the wreath more color. I even add a ficus leaf stem inside the cornucopia.

There are many ways to be creative with a cornucopia and several arrangements you can design to flow from it. A pumpkin, grapes, a banana, a pear, carrots, eggplant, and even some natural-colored filler flower flowing out in different directions make a colorful and abundant cornucopia.

To help secure the fruits and vegetables, I tuck a small piece of desert foam into the cornucopia and glue it in. Then, I insert the picks attached to my pumpkins, gourds, and fruits. I know they will stay in place. Cover the opening with pretty green moss to hide the desert foam and you're all set.

For even more visual interest, I love to add some everyday flowers and colors, such as these beautiful hydrangeas, to the usual yellows, browns, and oranges of fall.

A large, full, glorious bow is the icing on the cake when it comes to wreaths. A bow can add to the theme of a wreath, its colors perfectly complementing the other elements you have chosen. I make several different types of bows for my wreaths; single ribbon, double ribbon, triple ribbon—even a single ribbon bow with two smaller bows added to make it look like a double ribbon bow!

Rolls of ribbon inspire me and enhance my creative side. I always keep a large selection of ribbons in many materials and colors right at my fingertips. There are wired burlaps, denims, and cottons along with mesh, sheer, and deco. I keep many solids on hand because they look great mixed with plaid, polka dot, and chevron in double and triple ribbon bows.

One side of my studio is filled with more rolls of ribbon than I can count, and I have more stored away in clear containers to bring out for each season or until I have time

to use them all! These choices encourage me as I brainstorm and plan wreath designs. Solids, patterns, and colors look so pretty together. I love to hold up different styles, patterns, and textures against my wreath to decide which will pop with the right color combination.

The size ribbon I use the most is #9, approximately 1 ½" wide. The narrow width of this ribbon makes it so much easier to tie your own single, double, or even triple ribbon bow.

I do use the wider #40 ribbons at Christmastime. There is nothing more beautiful than a bright red bow with several long streamers enhancing an evergreen Christmas wreath.

A word of advice on ribbon: Don't ever purchase ribbon that isn't wired. You'll have to take my word for this one. The only time you will find me making a bow out of a ribbon without wire is at Christmas, when I'm using the outdoor red velvet ribbon which is stiff because of the outdoor backing.

To make the process of bow-making easier, do yourself a favor and let go of the idea that the ribbon should be rolled up nicely while you're experimenting. Holding a bow in your hand while tying it and continually having to unroll it at the same time is impossible. I unroll six to eight yards of ribbon, let it fall to the floor so nothing restricts it as I begin tying my bows.

Nancy's Bow Recipe

I was never a huge fan of the way everyone else tied their bows. The only solution was to develop a method that was different and unique. Now, no one else ties bows like I do.

When I had my storefront business, I taught bow-making classes. My students often found it difficult to master the steps. I devised an easy solution and it came to be known as a "Nancy" bow. This unique, easy-to-follow recipe seemed to break the barrier faced by many when it came to bow making. The photo below gives you a visual reference to follow as we go through the steps in the process.

My easy-to-follow bow recipe is different than you have ever seen before, but it works. Everyone I have taught this method to has learned to tie beautiful, full bows with ease.

How to Tie a Double Ribbon Bow

After unrolling my ribbon into a pile on the floor, I begin with a streamer about 30" to 36" (76 to 91 cm) long.

1. I measure streamers from both ribbons I am using for this particular bow. I begin by holding the two ribbons together, with the plaid on top of the hot pink. I hold the streamers pointing toward my body, pinch them together in the middle, then pull the longer end with the two ribbons out and away from my body, taking them around and under, and then bringing them back toward me.

The motion I follow is "away, down, under, and back." After bringing it back toward me, I pinch it together. There—I have my first loop!

2. The second loop is formed like the first loop. I bring the ribbons (still holding them one on top of the other) toward my body, down, under, and away from me; ready to pinch and twist.

These two loops should now look like a bow tie or a shoestring bow. They are directly opposite each other and exactly the same length. I placed the plaid on top in the first loop, and twist it throughout to be sure it stays on the top during the rest of the bow-making process. The longer ribbon I measured before beginning is streamer #1 in the bow recipe on page 86.

3. After completing the first layer, I begin adding loops to my second layer. This layer is shaped like an X and consists of four loops that are the exact same length. The loops of the second layer are numbered #4, #5, #6, and #7. The length of these four loops should be about 1" to 1½" (2.5 to 4 cm) longer than the first layer of the bow tie.

I begin by going to the left of my bow after twisting and turning the ribbon. I run my fingers along the loop as I pull it out away from my body, bring it around, down, and underneath, and then back toward my body.

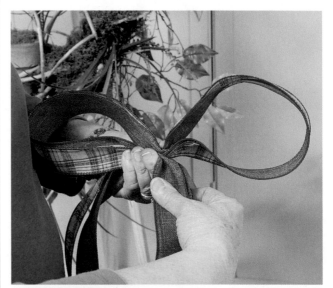

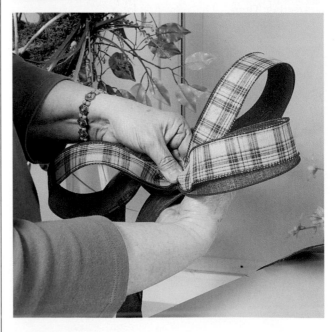

These first two loops create the top or front of your bow, the bow tie, with loops on both sides. Referring to the bow recipe, the first loop of the bow tie is #2, and the second loop of the bow tie is #3. Each layer hereafter is formed working away from you and toward the floor. We are layering sets of loops, with each layer getting fuller and a little longer.

It's important to hold the center section of the bow tightly throughout the process. I do lift up a finger or two on my left hand (the hand that is holding it) in order to add and hold the twisted section where the loops meet in the middle. I pinch, twist, and lay my fingers back down.

Before I pinch or twist this loop, I compare the bow tie loop in the first layer to the first loop of the X in the second layer. I make sure that the bow tie loop is around 1½" (4 cm) shorter than the loop of the X.

To successfully bring it directly opposite the first loop, the second loop has to point to the right side of the bow tie. I pinch and twist again.

4. Next, I pinch and twist the loop in such a way that it makes the third loop of the X. It points to the right of my first bow tie loop. I bring it away from my body, wrap around, underneath, and back toward me. This loop should also be 1½" (4 cm) longer than the bow tie in the first layer. Remember, each loop in the X layer should be exactly the same length.

I follow the same steps when creating the last loop of this layer. I bring it toward my body, around, and underneath. This loop will go out of the left side of the second loop of my bow tie.

Notice in the photo that you can easily see the bow tie in the middle and the four loops of the X. Honestly, that's all there is to it. You can stop there if you don't need a really full bow.

5. For wreath bows, especially those with two ribbons, I make the bow tie, an X, another bow tie, and finish with one loop curling up out of the top. So, when we have our bow tie and X completed, I start on the third layer, another bow tie.

Remember, the bow tie goes straight down the middle. The bow tie loops in this layer are #8 and #9 in the recipe photo. Form them by going back and forth in the very center of the bow. These loops don't ever go out to the sides like the loops of the X. As I am forming the first loop of this bow tie, I bring it out and away from me with the two ribbons still on top of each other. They are pulled around, underneath, and back toward my body.

Again, I stop and compare the loop to one of the loops of the X to make sure it is also around 1" to 1½" (2.5 to 4 cm) longer. Each additional layer should be approximately that much longer.

I pinch it together, twist, make the first loop of the bow tie, twist again, and bring it toward my body, around, underneath, and back toward the center. That gives me the third layer, or the second bow tie.

If I were using a single ribbon instead of a double, I would probably add another X to add a few more loops to this bow. But when I separate the pink and plaid ribbons within this double ribbon bow, you'll see that I have twice as many loops.

The Top Loop in a Bow

The loop that comes straight out at the top of the bow and comes back down to form my second streamer is very important, and it's probably the hardest one to learn. It gives an extra loop pointing out the top of the bow. You don't want to have an empty space that looks like there should be a loop. It fills a gap you would otherwise have. I don't ever like to twist and pull on my loops too much in order to fill in an empty space where there should be a loop. It is much easier to place your loops exactly where they are needed. That is another thing you'll find different about a Nancy bow.

After following all of the previous steps, you should have a bow tie, an X, a bow tie, then one odd loop that sticks up at the top of the bow. See how I came straight up with the single loop from the left side? Don't twist it quite yet, but simply make a loop that will flow toward the back of the bow. After making the loop, twist it and have it hang down the left side of your bow. This will create your second set of streamers. The top loop is #10 and the last streamer is #11 in the bow recipe.

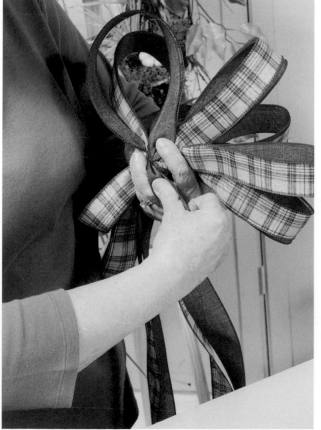

When the top loop has been added, and all the loops are relatively even, the next step is to tie off the bow, using a pipe cleaner, or a chenille stem.

Tying Off a Bow

I've experimented with tying bows off in many different ways, and I've found that the best thing to use is a chenille stem or a pipe cleaner instead of wire that can cut your fingers. I use the moss green color for all of my bows.

While I am still holding my bow together in my left hand, I bend a pipe cleaner in half with my right hand. I thread the pipe cleaner in between the two fingers on my left hand and bring the other side into the middle of the top loop.

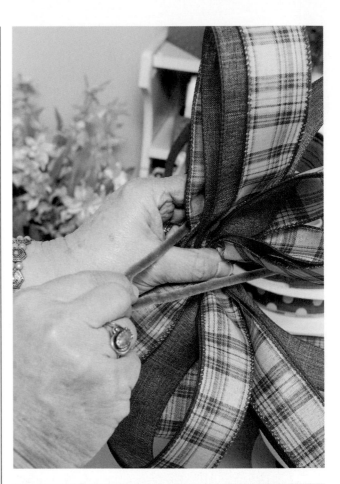

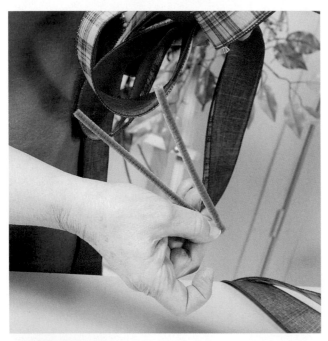

With my right index finger and thumb I twist, putting a lot of pressure on the two pipe cleaners. I then pull tightly and twist both hands in opposite directions as I go.

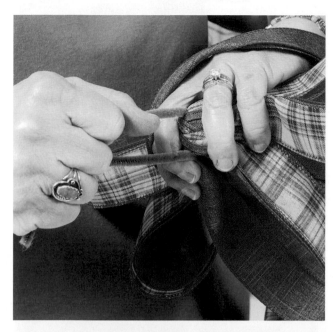

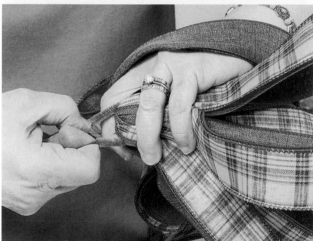

If the bow is tied correctly and tightly, you'll be able to pull and twist on your bow's loops without altering any of the lengths so that it stays proportionate.

Once the bow is all tied together, the top loop will be sticking straight up. One streamer is on the right side of the pipe cleaner and the other is where the loops come back down on the left side of the pipe cleaner. If you follow these instructions, your bow should look like this.

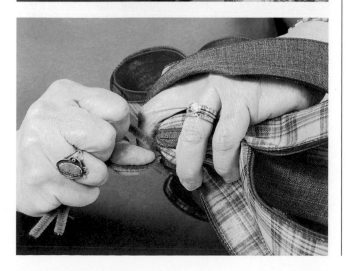

Although it's lovely the way it is, with hot pink peeking out from under the plaid ribbon, it looks even more beautiful once you separate the pink and plaid ribbons.

Separating Ribbons in a Double Ribbon Bow

I begin this process by holding the bow against my body and reaching deep into the center of the bow, where it's tied together. I pull the pink ribbon out from inside the plaid, twisting each loop in opposite directions to make sure they will not slide back together.

One ribbon goes toward my body and the other goes in the opposite direction. Remember, the twist is important because it keeps the plaid ribbon on top of the solid throughout this process. It's pretty difficult to go wrong during this step, as long as your bow is tied as tightly as it should be.

Before separating the loops, I think about which direction I'm going to pull the solid ribbon out of the plaid so as to alternate the two different ribbons and colors as much as possible.

After I have separated the ribbon loops from each other, the bow is pretty, but it obviously needs "fluffing." To do this, I run my fingers along each wired side. Sometimes I stick my entire hand inside and twist back and forth with some pressure against the loop to open it up.

Curling the Streamers

The final step is trimming the streamers to the length you want, and then curling them so that they hang down and complement the bow perfectly. I run the streamer through my fingers, making sure I apply pressure on each side of the wired edges. As I pull my hand and fingers down, it slightly curls the streamers. It's important to curl all the way to the end of each streamer, twisting it around at the bottom.

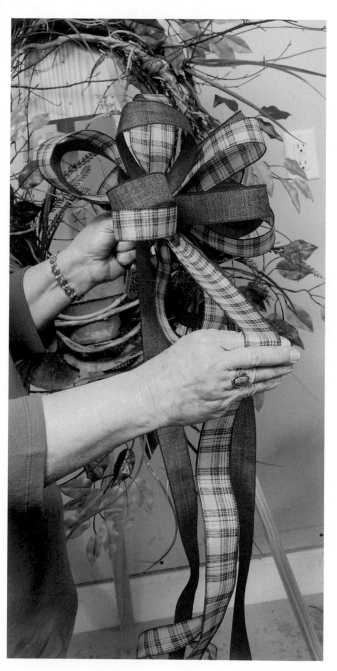

This double ribbon bow looks beautiful as I hold it up against my basic wreath. Do you notice the beautifully curled streamers hanging down? Such a gorgeous look!

Long, curling streamers add to the look. Resist the temptation to trim everything too neatly!

Single Ribbon Bow

This single ribbon bow is made with natural wired burlap. I begin the bow after unrolling my entire length of ribbon into a pile on the floor. Let's start with a streamer around 30" to 36" (76 to 91 cm) long.

1. We're going to use the same process as in the previous bow we made together. Holding the streamer pointing toward my body, I pinch it together in the middle, taking the longer end of the ribbon out and away from my body. I then pull it around, under, and back toward me. The motion I follow is "away, down, under, and back." After bringing it back toward me, I pinch and twist it together. That is the first loop.

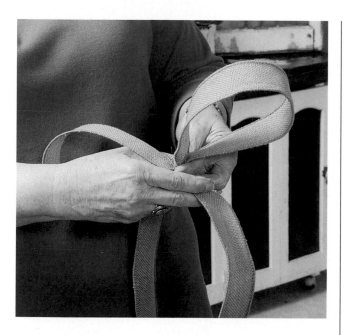

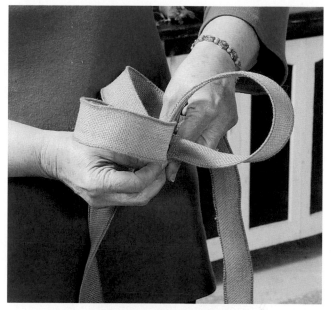

2. The second loop is formed exactly like the first loop, but in the opposite direction. For the second loop, I bring the ribbon toward my body, down, under, and then away from me. I twist and pinch it, making sure it is directly underneath the first pinch and twist.

These two loops should now look like a bow tie or a shoestring bow. They are directly opposite each other and exactly the same length.

These first two loops create the front or center of the bow as you are looking at it. The following loops will be layered underneath—never on top of—this bow tie layer. Each layer from here on is formed while working away from you and toward the floor.

It's important to hold the center section of the bow tightly throughout the process. I do lift up a finger or two on my left hand (the hand that is holding it) in order to add and hold the twisted sections where loops continually meet in the middle. I pinch, twist, and lay my fingers back down.

tip It's usually easier to work with lots of ribbon when making bows. You can always make smaller loops once you've learned the basic techniques.

3. After completing the first layer, I begin adding loops to my second layer. This layer is shaped in the form of an X and consists of four loops that are the exact same length. The length of these four loops should be about 1" to 1½" (2.5 to 4 cm) longer than the first layer or the bow tie. I begin this layer by going to the left of my bow after twisting and turning the ribbon. I run my fingers along the loop as I pull it out away from my body, around, down, and underneath.

Before I pinch or twist this loop, I compare the bow tie loop from the first layer to the first loop of the X in the second layer. I make sure that the bow tie loop is around 1½" (4 cm) shorter than the loop of the X.

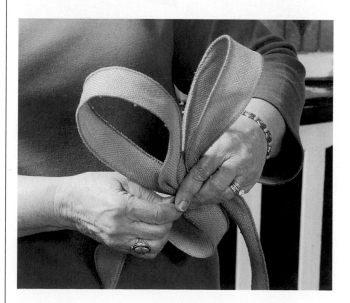

To successfully bring it directly opposite the first loop, the second loop has to point to the right side of the bow tie. I pinch and twist again.

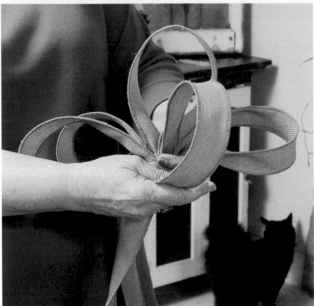

4. Next, I pinch and twist the loop in such a way that it makes the third loop of the X. It points to the right of my first bow tie loop. Pulling it away from my body, I wrap around, underneath, and back toward me. This loop should also be 1½" (4 cm) longer than the bow tie in the first layer. Remember, the four loops in the X should be exactly the same length. I follow the same steps when creating the last loop of this layer. I bring it toward my body, around, and underneath. This loop will go out of the left side of the second loop of my bow tie.

Notice in the photo that you can easily see the bow tie in the middle and the four loops of the X. Honestly, that's all there is to it. You can stop right there if you don't need a really full bow, but if you do, just continue this process over and over until the bow is full enough.

5. Are you ready to make another bow tie? The bow tie goes straight down the middle, just as before. It is formed by going back and forth in the very center of your bow. These loops don't ever go out to the sides like the X does. I think you can remember how to make the bow tie—just make sure it is 1" to 1½" longer than the loops of the X. Each layer gets longer and longer as you keep working away underneath the first bow tie.

We could add another X to make sure your bow is full, but I'm going to teach you a little trick with this bow, so we're going to finish it off with the single loop coming out of the top, just as we did with the double-ribbon bow.

After following all of the previous steps, you should have a bow tie, an X, another bow tie, another X, and then one odd loop sticking up out of the top. The single loop comes from the left side. You don't want to twist it quite yet. Simply make a loop that will flow toward the back of the bow. Give it a twist, and turn it so it will be the left streamer on your bow. This becomes your second streamer.

6. Tie the bow off tightly with a pipe cleaner and trim the streamers.

Adding Extra Streamers

Would you like extra streamers in this bow? It is so simple. Measure off a ribbon strip about 5' (1.5 m) long. Fold it in half, pinch it, and tie it with a pipe cleaner. Attach it to the wreath exactly where you'll be attaching your bow, and then tie the bow in right on top of it.

There are now four streamers. You can let them hang, or you can tuck them in where you might like them to fall. Each streamer will curl in its own direction, and if you let the loops of ribbon fall naturally so that you can see where they land, you'll get an idea of where they'll look the prettiest before you decide where to attach them.

I want to pinch one of the streamers and tuck it in between the mushrooms. I could easily pinch the ribbon, add a pick, and tuck it in. But there is an easier way I want to show you. This is a place where my Bostitch stapler comes in handy. I use it to staple the ribbon into a point. I then add a little glue to the stapled area and slide it right in between the mushrooms.

When working with hot glue in a tight space, I always grab one of my floral picks to help push it in. Look how beautiful it looks curling in between the mushrooms, and then flowing back out and down from the wreath.

Get the Look of a Double Ribbon Bow—The Easy Way

Would you like to make a single ribbon bow look as if you tied a double ribbon bow? I have a very simple solution for you: Tie two smaller bows, attach them to 6" (15.25 cm) picks, and insert them into the wreath on either side of your first bow.

Here, I am making the two smaller bows out of green mesh ribbon that is see-through. It's a very basic, wired texture ribbon that makes stiff loops.

Beginning with a fairly short streamer, make a bow tie, and then make only one half of the X. That adds up to be a total of four loops—two on each side of where they are tied—and two streamers. The best way to insert this second bow is to put it on a pick. Be sure to tie it with a pipe cleaner first. I cut off the pipe cleaner ends at different lengths; one is cut about 1½" (4 cm) long, and the second is a little bit longer. This just makes it easier to twist the wire tightly from the floral pick.

With the two pipe cleaners sticking out of the back of this bow, lay your pick beside the two pipe cleaner stems and twist the wire very tightly. I want that pick to come out as close to the middle of the bow as possible so it looks as if the entire bow was only tied once. But, we know better, don't we?

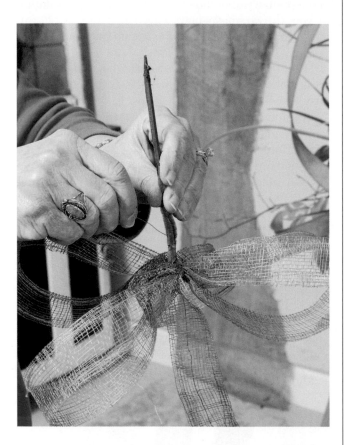

With the main, center bow already in place on your wreath, it's time to insert the two side bows. You now have two 6" picks holding smaller, identical bows. The first pick should be tucked in from the left and the other pick from the right.

Both picked bows should be inserted toward and under the main bow. The picks for the side bows will be pointing toward each other and meeting underneath the center bow.

With the tip of your glue gun, reach into the center, where the picks entered, and add some glue. You don't want the side bows pulling out.

Be patient as you pull and twist the loops where they need to go. The more you do that, the more it looks as if the bow was tied with two ribbons at once.

Your finished product suddenly looks like a complicated double ribbon bow!

Chapter 5
Christmas with Nancy

Christmas has always been a magical season in our family and, of course, for my business, which reflects the wonder and color of this very special time of year.

When I first started in the floral design business, I attended a major national wholesale market and was overwhelmed by the lights, the glitz, and the glamour. Christmas was everywhere! Since my first trip, over twenty-five years ago, my storefront business and now my online businesses are transformed each year to reflect the beauty of this very special season.

With my Christmas designs, I enjoy creating not only a look but a feeling of wonder and excitement for myself, my family, and my customers. You can do this with your floral designs, too. When you design a wreath from past Christmas memories coupled with the styles, supplies, and materials available to you today, you have the ability to fashion something unique.

Although I design natural, "wild and woodsy" wreaths throughout the year, I create many types, styles, and colors of Christmas wreaths. In fact, I really love the glittering, glistening look of twinkling lights reflecting on shiny

ornaments, ribbons, and poinsettias. For me, Christmas is a mix of many different styles. It is eclectic, it is glorious, and it is exciting.

Many of the tools, supplies, and techniques I have shared with you throughout this book can be used to create Christmas wreaths, and I won't repeat them here. In this chapter, I will show you some of my favorite Christmas "extras" and introduce you to working with evergreen wreaths.

Christmas Finery

Ornaments

I am as big a fan of glitzy, glamorous, shimmering, and sparkling Christmas designs as anyone else. I use them in my own home. During Christmas season, you would be hard-pressed to find a nook or corner of my home, shop, or pergola that didn't contain some of my most precious Christmas decorations. I love eye-catching, shining, and sparkling ornaments. They sparkle and shine hanging near or tucked around tiny white Christmas lights. Some have glitter or sequins, and some are iced. Others are bright and shiny, or covered in sparkles. The traditional Christmas colors of red, green, and white are definitely my favorites.

tip Don't ignore flea markets, antique malls, and yard sales in your quest to find great items to add to your holiday wreaths.

This glistening, glittering, glitzy wreath has adorned my front door for the last two Christmas seasons. Filling this large wreath with three different styles of shimmering ribbons made this design full even before I considered adding anything else. But there was much more to add. Many colors and styles of scrumptious ornaments and red and green fillers bring it to life along with some of the prettiest poinsettias I have ever seen.

Fruit

Another of my favorite holiday design elements, "sugared" fruit, can be used in natural or glitzy Christmas wreaths. The look is more subdued than sequined or iced fruit and is very much at home in a natural style wreath, but has enough sparkle to work in a "glam" wreath as well.

This wreath uses fruit, greenery, and a large, sumptuous, red burlap bow to convey the natural beauty and abundance of the holiday season.

Ribbons and Bows

Ribbons and bows make the wreath at Christmastime, and there is a huge assortment of types, styles, and colors of Christmas ribbon available at craft, hobby, and fabric stores. Don't be overwhelmed by them. Just enjoy them all!

I like to use #40 ribbon, measuring from 2¾" to 3" (7 to 8 cm), for my Christmas decorating. The wider ribbon against a green Christmas wreath adds to that full, lush look of Christmas that we all love. If you find a narrower #9 ribbon that you like, just be sure to add more loops than you would with #40 ribbon. You'll still end up with a full and gorgeous bow—especially when you use my bow recipe!

Christmas Wreath Forms

This wreath mixes narrow and wide ribbon, printed and solid, to bring the Christmas glow to your door.

I also like to use more streamers at Christmas. If you don't have many materials such as flowers, berries, or other items to add to your wreath, it is easy to make it look full by filling it with ribbons and streamers. You'll have a large and showy wreath, like this one, for a small investment.

I am devoted to my wild birch wreath bases all through the year, but at Christmas my favorite base is the old standby evergreen wreath. Designing a Christmas wreath on a wired artificial evergreen base is fast and easy, and there are many different kinds available—some with mixed greens, pine cones, berry clusters, and other ornamentation—at a wide range of prices.

The nicer, more expensive wreath forms are fuller, with more greenery, but since I add so much to my Christmas wreaths, I usually use the less expensive type.

All artificial green Christmas wreath forms are filled with green wired extensions that are mashed tightly against the wreath when it is purchased. Since they are flat, some fluffing is required. (Fluffing is a word you'll get used to when working with floral and wreath design!)

This process is quick. I reach inside, pulling and straightening each extension as I work my way around the wreath. I straighten each one, making sure they point in different directions and are not standing up straight. Some should point up, others to the outside of the wreath, and others into the middle. When finished, you have a nice full wreath that is ready to be filled with gorgeous ribbons, ornaments, flowers, and fillers.

Besides fluffing you can plump up a scrawny wreath by adding some additional greens. I keep inexpensive Christmas garlands and greens—often purchased at reduced prices after the holidays—on hand for this purpose. I look for pieces that have a wide mix of greens such as white pine, cedar, Scotch pine, and pine cones.

I cut the garlands into 8" to 10" (20 to 25 cm) sections. These types of stems can be hard to cut as many thick wires run down the center, so you may need your extra-large wire cutters for this job.

tip Many of the cheaper artificial evergreen wreath forms may have only one or sometimes two wired circles holding the green extensions together. Most of the more expensive ones are put together with two or even three circles of wire. If you were to lay the less expensive wreath flat on a surface, you'd see the wired circles touching the surface.

If you were to lay the nicer, more expensive wreaths with two or more circles of wire flat on a surface, you'd see the inside circle does not rest flatly. It is raised higher, adding more depth and fullness to the wreath. Even though I look for less-expensive Christmas evergreen wreaths with a mix of greens, I do like the ones with more than one layer of wire.

Attaching these pieces of garland into the wreath is easy—no hot glue, wire, or pipe cleaners are needed. Remember I explained how the extensions coming out of the wreath are wired? Simply twist these wired pieces around ornament hooks, flowers, signs, berry stems and anything else you are adding to your wreath to make it secure. I am adding four garland pieces to help this wreath look full and lush.

This wreath is what I would consider a natural holiday wreath. Its base is an evergreen Christmas wreath form like everyone uses during the holidays. The only difference is that you don't really see this wreath form, do you? You do see the long needle pine that I added, along with long leaf stems such as ficus, eucalyptus, and smaller, leafy fillers similar to boxwood.

The red and tan burlap chevron ribbon is not a Christmas ribbon, it is an everyday ribbon—meaning I use this one year round. The fact that it is placed on an evergreen wreath gives it a Christmas feel. Clusters of small red berries are the right color for the season, but they look more natural since they lack the shine and glitter of some Christmas berries.

Does it matter that I'm not using Christmas fruit and berries? No, absolutely not. I love the mix and colors of everyday fruits and veggies like the pomegranate, carrots, pears, lemons, oranges, and apples.

For the final Christmas wreath in this book, I'll return to my "wild and woodsy" roots, adding variegated mini-leaf ivy, long blade grasses, a large mix of Christmas greens, and a long leafy stem of ficus, along with a 6" (15.25 cm) wide red burlap ribbon, fruits, and berries.

I've also added another natural element not often thought of—natural colored mushrooms. They give this wreath that woodsy look for which I am known.

For a final touch of nature, I've added pine cones, which are plentiful here in South Carolina. They can be found in baskets in my shop during most seasons. I am particularly partial to the long, skinny, slightly-curved white pine cones. These naturally have white tips which show up well in Christmas designs.

If you love decorating for Christmas as much as I do, you'll love watching what I do to spruce up the house at

www.LadybugWreaths.com/videotraining

A Final Word from Nancy

I have truly enjoyed leading you on this delightful journey into the world of wreath design. I've shared many of my techniques, designs, and secrets that it took me many years to perfect.

It is my prayer that you'll find that very special gift from deep within while realizing you have found a hobby you love. Wreath making can lead you on the journey of your dreams.

When I began designing wreaths, never in a million years did I realize it could make such a huge difference in my life. Never did I realize this could grow into the profitable business it has.

It wasn't that long ago that I needed a purpose for my life. Fibromyalgia and Celiac disease had taken that away from me. I had no confidence in myself or my abilities. Learning and perfecting a hobby I love has filled my heart and my life with joy and a sense of fulfillment.

It is my desire that you wake up each morning with a start—one that makes you jump out of bed to do something you love. May each day be filled with color, design, and beauty.

I am blessed to be able to introduce you to a hobby that can add so much beauty to your life.

Smiles and blessings,
Nancy